THE CHARACTER AND LOGICAL METHOD OF POLITICAL ECONOMY

Also Published in

Reprints of Economic Classics

BY JOHN E. CAIRNES

ESSAYS ON POLITICAL ECONOMY [1873]

AN EXAMINATION INTO THE PRINCIPLES OF
CURRENCY INVOLVED IN THE BANK CHARTER
ACT OF 1844 [1854]

THE
CHARACTER

AND

LOGICAL METHOD

OF

POLITICAL ECONOMY

BY

JOHN E. CAIRNES

[1875, 2nd Edition 1888]

REPRINTS OF ECONOMIC CLASSICS

AUGUSTUS M. KELLEY · PUBLISHER
NEW YORK · 1965

FIRST PUBLISHED 1875
2ND EDITION 1888

REPRINTED 1965

LIBRARY OF CONGRESS CATALOGUE CARD NUMBER
65 - 20922

THE

CHARACTER AND LOGICAL METHOD

OF

POLITICAL ECONOMY.

By J. E. CAIRNES, LL.D.

EMERITUS PROFESSOR OF POLITICAL ECONOMY IN UNIVERSITY COLLEGE, LONDON,
AUTHOR OF "SOME LEADING PRINCIPLES OF POLITICAL
ECONOMY, NEWLY EXPOUNDED."

London:

MACMILLAN AND CO.

1888.

PREFACE TO SECOND EDITION.

In offering to the public a new edition of some lectures delivered in Dublin more than seventeen years ago, a few words of explanation are needed. As regards the substance of the opinions advanced — the view taken of Political Economy, and of its methods of proof and development—the present work does not differ from its predecessor; but extensive changes have been made in the form and treatment. Numerous passages have been recast; increased prominence has been given to aspects of the case only touched on in the former volume; and some entirely new topics have been introduced. To one of these—"Definition"—an additional lecture has been devoted. I would fain hope that in its new shape the work will be found somewhat less unworthy than in its earlier form of such favor as it has met with. No one, however, can be more conscious than the author how very far it still falls short of what such a work ought to be.

In connection with logical method, a good deal of discussion has of late taken place on a question that had been but little heard of when the book first appeared—I mean the employment of Mathematics in the development of economic doctrine. The position then taken with reference to this point was that, having regard to the sources from which Political Economy derives its premises, the science does not admit of mathematical treatment. Since that time, my friend Professor Jevons has published an able work ("The Theory of Political Economy"), in which the opposite opinion is maintained; and some few others, both here and on the Continent of Europe, have followed in his track. Having weighed Professor Jevons's argument to the best of my ability, and so far as this was possible for one unversed in Mathematics, I still adhere to my original view. So far as I can see, economic truths are not discoverable through the instrumentality of Mathematics. If this view be unsound, there is at hand an easy means of refutation—the production of an economic truth, not before known, which has been thus arrived at; but I am not aware that up to the present any such evidence has been furnished of the efficacy of the mathematical method. In taking this ground, I have no desire to deny that it may be possible to employ geometrical diagrams or mathematical formulæ for the purpose of exhibiting economic doctrines *reached by other paths;* and it may be that there are minds for which this mode of presenting the subject has advantages. What I venture to deny is the doctrine

which Professor Jevons and others have advanced—
that economic knowledge can be extended by such
means ; that Mathematics can be applied to the development of economic truth, as it has been applied to the
development of mechanical and physical truth ; and,
unless it can be shown either that mental feelings admit of being expressed in precise quantitative forms,
or, on the other hand, that economic phenomena do not
depend upon mental feelings, I am unable to see how
this conclusion can be avoided. "The laws of Political Economy," says Mr. Jevons, "must be mathematical
for the most part, because they deal with quantities and
the relations of quantities." If I do not mistake, something more than this is needed to sustain Mr. Jevons's
position.

I have retained most of the discussions in the original
notes, although some of the questions discussed have lost
much of the practical interest they once had ; what was
formerly speculation having in some instances become
realized fact. They will not on this account, however,
serve less well the purpose of their first introduction—
that of illustrating the principles of economic method.

It falls to me once again to have to express my deep
obligations to my friend Professor Nesbitt, who, with his
usual kindness in correcting the proofs, has not a little
lightened my present labors.   J. E. CAIRNES.

KIDBROOK PARK ROAD, S.E., *Feb.*, 1875.

PREFACE TO FIRST EDITION.

ONE of the conditions attached to the Whately Professorship of Political Economy requires that at least one lecture in the year shall be published by the Professor. In the following pages I have ventured considerably to exceed this requirement, the subject which I selected as most appropriate for my opening course not being such as could be conveniently compressed within a single lecture.

With respect to the views advanced in this work, it may be well, in order to prevent misapprehension, to disclaim at the outset all pretense to the enunciation of any *new* method of conducting economic inquiries. My aim, on the contrary, has been to bring back the discussions of Political Economy to those tests and standards which were formerly considered the ultimate criteria of economic doctrine, but which have been completely lost sight of in many modern publications. With a view to this, I have endeavored to ascertain and clearly to state the character of Political Economy, as this science appears to have been conceived by that succession of writers of which Smith, Malthus, Ricardo, and Mill are the most distinguished names; and from the character thus ascertained to deduce the logical method appropriate thereto; while I have sought further to fortify the conclusions to which I have been led by the analogy of the method which in the physical sciences has been fruitful of such remarkable results."

It may, perhaps, be thought that it would have conduced more to the advantage of economic science if, instead of pausing to investigate the logical principles involved in its doctrines, I had turned those principles to practical account by directing investigation into new regions. To this I can only reply that the contrarieties of opinion at present prevailing among writers on Political Economy are so numerous and so fundamental, that, as it seems to me, no other escape is open to economists, from the confusion and the contradictions in which the science is involved, than by a recurrence to those primary considerations by which the importance of doctrines and the value of evidence are to be determined. To disregard this conflict of opinion, and to proceed to develop principles the foundations of which are constantly impugned, would be to prosecute inquiry to little purpose.

The discussion of economic method with a view to this object has rendered it necessary for me to refer principally to those questions on which opinion is at present divided; and in doing so I have been led frequently to quote from recent writers for the purpose simply of dissenting from their doctrines. This course, which I would gladly have avoided had it been compatible with the end in view, has given to portions of these lectures more of a controversial character than is, perhaps, desirable.

I feel also that some apology is due for the number and the length of the notes. As I have just stated, the nature of the subject required frequent reference to disputed topics. To have met the current objections to the principles which I assumed by stopping on each occasion to discuss them in the text, would have inconveniently broken the sequence of ideas, and hopelessly weakened the force of the general argument. On the other hand, to have wholly passed them by without notice would, perhaps, have been still more unsatisfactory to those who were disposed to adopt such objections. I should thus have been guilty of the imprudence of a commander who invades a country leaving numerous untaken fortresses in his rear. Under these circumstances I have had recourse to the only other alternative—that of transferring such discussions to the notes, or, where the argument is too long for a note, to an appendix.

*　　*　　*　　*　　*　　*

J. E. CAIRNES.

A 2

CONTENTS.

LECTURE I.

INTRODUCTORY.

LECTURE II.

OF THE MENTAL AND PHYSICAL PREMISES OF POLITICAL
ECONOMY, AND OF THE LOGICAL CHARACTER OF
THE DOCTRINES THENCE DEDUCED.

LECTURE III.

OF THE LOGICAL METHOD OF POLITICAL ECONOMY.

LECTURE IV.

OF THE LOGICAL METHOD OF POLITICAL ECONOMY.—
(*Continued.*)

LECTURE V.

OF THE SOLUTION OF AN ECONOMIC PROBLEM, AND OF THE DEGREE OF PERFECTION OF WHICH IT IS SUSCEPTIBLE.

LECTURE VI.

OF THE PLACE AND PURPOSE OF DEFINITION IN POLITICAL ECONOMY.

LECTURE VII.

OF THE MALTHUSIAN DOCTRINE OF POPULATION.

LECTURE VIII.

OF THE THEORY OF RENT.

APPENDICES.

THE

CHARACTER AND LOGICAL METHOD

OF

POLITICAL ECONOMY.

THE CHARACTER AND LOGICAL METHOD

POLITICAL ECONOMY.

LECTURE I.

INTRODUCTORY.

§ 1. In commencing a course of lectures on Political
Economy, it is usual and natural to indulge in some con-
gratulatory remarks on the progress of the science in recent times, and more particularly on the satisfactory results which have attended the extensive, though as yet
but partial, recognition of its principles in the commercial and financial codes of the country. It is, indeed, not
easy to exaggerate the importance of these latter achievements, and it is certainly true that economic doctrines
have in recent years received some useful developments
and corrections; at the same time I think it must be admitted that, on the whole, the present condition and
prospects of the science are not such as a political economist can contemplate with unmixed satisfaction.

It is now a quarter of a century since Colonel Torrens
wrote as follows: " In the progress of the human mind,
a period of controversy among the cultivators of any
branch of science must necessarily precede the period

of unanimity.   With respect to Political Economy, the period of controversy is passing away, and that of unanimity rapidly approaching.   Twenty years hence there will scarcely exist a doubt respecting any of its fundamental principles." [1]   Five-and-thirty years have now passed since this unlucky prophecy was uttered, and yet such questions as those respecting the laws of population, of rent, of foreign trade, the effects of different kinds of expenditure upon distribution, the theory of prices—all fundamental in the science—are still unsettled, and must still be considered as " open questions," if that expression may be applied to propositions which are still vehemently debated, not merely by sciolists and smatterers, who may always be expected to wrangle, but by the professed cultivators and recognized expounders of the science. [2]   So far from the period of controversy having passed, it seems hardly yet to have begun — controversy, I mean, not merely respecting propositions of secondary importance, or the practical application of scientific doctrines (for such controversy is only an evidence of the vitality of a science, and is a necessary condition of its progress), but controversy respecting fundamental principles which lie at the root of its reasonings, and which were regarded as settled when Colonel Torrens wrote.

This state of instability and uncertainty as to fundamental propositions is certainly not favorable to the successful cultivation of Political Economy—it is not possible to raise a solid or durable edifice upon shifting quicksands ; besides, the danger is ever imminent of re-

---

[1] " Essay on the Production of Wealth," Introduction, p. xiii.   1821.

[2] *Vide* Appendix A.

viving that skepticism respecting all economic speculation which at one time so much impeded its progress.
It would, indeed, be vain to expect that Political Economy should be as rapidly and steadily progressive as the
mathematical and physical sciences. Its close affinity
to the moral sciences, as has been often pointed out,
brings it constantly into collision with moral feelings
and prepossessions which can scarcely fail to make themselves felt in the discussion of its principles; while its
conclusions, intimately connected as they are with the
art of government, have a direct and visible bearing
upon human conduct in some of the most exciting pur-
suits of life. Add to this that the technical terms of
Political Economy are all taken from popular language,
and inevitably partake, in a greater or less degree, of
the looseness of colloquial usage. It is not, therefore,
to be expected that economic discussions should be carried on with the same singleness of purpose, or severity
of expression and argumentation — consequently with
the same success — as if they treated of the ideas of
number and extension, or of the properties of the material universe.

Such considerations will, no doubt, account for much
of the instability and vicissitude which have marked the
progress of economic inquiry; but I do not think they
are sufficient to explain the present vacillating and unsatisfactory condition of the science in respect to fundamental principles. To understand this, I think we must
advert to circumstances of a more special character, and
more particularly to the effect which the practical successes achieved by Political Economy (as exemplified in
the rapid and progressive extension of the commerce of

the country since the adoption of free trade) have had on the method of treating economic questions.

When Political Economy had nothing to recommend it to public notice but its own proper and intrinsic evidence, no man professed himself a political economist who had not conscientiously studied and mastered its elementary principles; and no one who acknowledged himself a political economist discussed an economic problem without constant reference to the recognized axioms of the science. But when the immense success of free trade gave experimental proof of the justice of those principles on which economists relied, an observable change took place both in the mode of conducting economic discussions, and in the class of persons who attached themselves to the cause of Political Economy. Many now enrolled themselves as political economists who had never taken the trouble to study the elementary principles of the science ; and some, perhaps, whose capacities did not enable them to appreciate its evidence ; while even those who had mastered its doctrines, in their anxiety to propitiate a popular audience, were too often led to abandon the true grounds of the science, in order to find for it in the facts and results of free trade a more popular and striking vindication.[1]   It was as if mathematicians, in order to attract new adherents to their ranks, had consented to abandon the method of analysis, and to rest the

---

[1] See an article in the *Edinburgh Review*, April, 1854, on "The Consumption of Food in the United Kingdom," and compare this with the celebrated "Merchants' Petition" of 1820, the production of Mr. Tooke. With reference to the former I may quote the remark of Mr. Tooke : "It is necessary, even in setting forth the successes of a just policy, that no violence should be done to established modes of reasoning, or to the facts of the case as they really exist."

truth of their formulas on the correspondence of the almanacs with astronomical events. The severe and logical style which characterized the cultivators of the science in the early part of the century has thus been changed to suit the different character of the audience to whom economists now address themselves. The discussions of Political Economy have been constantly assuming more of a statistical character; results are now appealed to instead of principles; the rules of arithmetic are superseding the canons of inductive reasoning;[1] till the true course of investigation has been well-nigh forgotten, and Political Economy seems in danger of realizing the fate of Atalanta,

"Declinat cursus, aurumque volubile tollit."

It has been remarked by Mr. Mill that "in whatever science there exist, among those who have attended to the subject, what are commonly called differences of principle, as distinguished from differences of matter of

---

[1] The error as to method complained of is the opposite of that of "anticipatio naturæ," which was the bane of science when Bacon wrote, and against which his most vigorous attacks were directed. Nevertheless (and it is a proof as well of the philosophic sagacity for which he was so distinguished, as of the perfect sobriety of his mind), the great reformer was not so carried away by his opposition to the prevailing abuse as to overlook the danger of its opposite. In the following passage he describes with singular accuracy both the error itself, to which I have adverted, and the causes of it. "Quod si etiam scientiam quandam, et dogmata ex experimentis moliantur; tamen semper fere studio præpropero et intempestivo deflectunt ad praxin: non tantum propter usum et fructum ejusmodi praxeos; sed ut in opere aliquo novo veluti pignus sibi arripiant, se non inutiliter in reliquis versaturos: *atque etiam aliis se venditent, ad existimationem meliorem comparandam de iis in quibus occupati sunt.* Ita fit, ut, more Atalantæ, de via decedant ad tollendum aureum pomum; interim vero cursum interrumpant, et victoriam emittant e manibus."—"Novum Organum," lib. i. aph. 70.

fact or detail, the cause will be found to be a difference in their conceptions of the philosophic method of the science. The parties who differ are guided, either knowingly or unconsciously, by different views concerning the nature of the evidence appropriate to the subject."[1] Now this appears to me to be strikingly the case with respect to those " differences of principle" to which I have adverted as at present existing among economists; and, therefore, I think I can not better carry out the views of the liberal founder of this chair than by availing myself of the opportunity which the opening of this course affords of considering at some length the nature, object, and limits of economic science, and the method of investigation proper to it as a subject of scientific study.

In discussing the nature, limits, and proper method of Political Economy, I shall at once pass over those numerous prepossessions connected with the study of this science—some of a moral, some of a religious, and some of a psychological nature—which so much impeded its early advances. To enter at any length into such considerations would be to occupy your time in traveling over ground which probably you have already traversed, or which, at all events, it is in your power to traverse, in other and more edifying company; and to waste my own in combating objections which either have ceased to exist, or, if they still exist, exist in spite of repeated refutations—refutations the most complete and irrefragable, to which I could hope to add nothing of point or weight, and which I should only weaken by translating them into my own language.[2]

---

[1] " Essays on some Unsettled Questions of Political Economy," p. 141.
[2] See particularly Whately's " Introd. Lectures on Political Economy."

I shall, therefore, at starting take it for granted that " wealth," the subject-matter of Political Economy, *is* susceptible of scientific treatment; that there *are* laws of its production and distribution ; that mankind in their industrial operations are *not* governed by mere caprice and accident, but by motives which act extensively and constantly—which may, therefore, be discovered and classified, and made to serve as the principles of subsequent deductions. I shall further take it for granted that a knowledge of these laws of the production and distribution of wealth is a desirable and useful acquisition, both as a part of a liberal education, and for the practical purposes to which it may be applied ; and, further, that this knowledge is more likely to be obtained by careful and systematic inquiry than by what is called the common-sense of practical men—another name for the crude guesses of unmethodized experience ; and, lastly, I shall assume that the study of those principles and motives of human conduct which are brought into play in the pursuit of wealth is not incompatible with the sentiments and duties of religion and morality.

§ 2. The question of the proper definition of Political Economy will come more fitly under our consideration after we have ascertained with some precision the character of the inquiry—that is to say, its purpose and the conditions under which this is sought to be accomplished. Even here, however, it may be well to refer to so much as may be fairly said to be agreed upon in connection with the subject of definition—agreed upon not indeed by all who discourse on economic questions (for on what are they agreed ?), but at least by the school of economists of whom Adam Smith may be regarded as the founder, and J. S. Mill as the latest and most distinguished expositor. So far as I know, all writers of this school, however they may differ as to the primary assumptions of Political Economy, or the method by which it ought to be cultivated, at least agree in describing it as the Science of Wealth. Now this implies agreement upon other points of considerable importance to which I desire to call your attention.

According to this view, then, you will observe that wealth constitutes the proper and exclusive subject-matter of Political Economy — that alone with which it is primarily and directly concerned. The various objections of a popular kind which have been advanced against the study upon the ground, as it has been phrased, of its "exclusive devotion to wealth," it is not my intention to notice at any length, for reasons which have been already assigned. I shall only remark that these objections almost all resolve themselves into this—that there are matters of importance which are not included within the range of Political Economy—an objection which seems to proceed upon the assumption that Political Economy is intended as a general curriculum of education, and not as a means of eliciting truths of a specific kind.[1] Thus a late writer in the *North British Review* speaks

---

[1] "Que l'économie politique ne s'occupe que des intérêts de cette vie, c'est une chose évidente, avouée. Chaque science a son objet qui lui est propre. Si elle sortait de ce monde, ce ne serait plus de l'économie politique, ce serait la théologie. On ne doit pas plus lui demander compte de ce qui se passe dans une monde meilleur, qu'on ne doit demander à la physiologie comment s'opère la digestion dans l'estomac des anges."— "Cours Complet d'Économie Politique," par J. B. Say, tom. i. p. 48, troisième édition.

slightingly of Political Economy as "a fragmentary science." Now what is the value of this objection? Does the writer mean that Political Economy is a fragment of universal knowledge? This may be granted, and yet the point of the objection be still not very apparent, unless we suppose that he designed to advocate some "great and comprehensive science," such as that which Thales and his contemporaries had in view when they inquired, "What is the origin of all things?" Indeed, if the history of scientific progress teach any lesson more distinctly than another, it is that human research has generally been successful just in proportion as its objects have been strictly limited and clearly defined; that is to say, in proportion as science has become "fragmentary."

Passing by popular objections, it can not be denied that the limitation of Political Economy to the single subject of wealth—or, to state the same idea in a different form, the constitution of a distinct science for the exclusive investigation of the class of phenomena called economic—has been objected to by writers of authority and reputation. Perhaps the most distinguished of those who have taken this view has been M. Comte. According to him all the various phenomena presented by society—political, jural, religious, educational, artistic, as well as economic—ought to be comprised within the range of a single inquiry, of which no one branch or portion ought to be studied except in constant connection with all the rest. I have elsewhere discussed this doctrine of M. Comte's at considerable length, and need not, therefore, do more than refer to it here.[1] Other writers, how-

---

[1] See "Essays in Political Economy, Theoretical and Applied."—M. Comte and Political Economy.

ever, of whom M. Say is one, without adopting this extreme view, have desired to extend the boundaries of economic investigation beyond the limits prescribed by the ordinary definition, and would embrace in the same discussion with the phenomena of wealth a large portion at least of the facts presented by man's moral and social nature. But the objections to this course appear to me to be fundamental and insuperable.

In the first place, the great variety of interests and considerations included under the science as thus conceived would seem to render the comprehension of them in one system of doctrines difficult, if not impracticable. But the fundamental defect in this mode of treatment —in the attempt to combine in the same discussion the laws of wealth and the laws, or a portion of the laws, of the moral and social nature of man—consists in this, that even where the subject-matter of the two inquiries is identical, even where the facts which they consider are the same, yet the relations and aspects under which these facts are viewed are essentially different. The same things, the same persons, the same actions are discussed with reference to a different object, and, therefore, require to be classified on a different principle.

If our object, for example, were to discover the laws of the production and distribution of wealth, those instruments of production the productiveness of which depends on the same conditions, and those persons whose share in the products of industry is governed by the same principles, should, respectively, be placed in the same categories; while, if our object were the larger one of social interests and relations generally, we might require a very different arrangement. Thus superior mental power, regarded with a view to the production of wealth, is an instrument of production perfectly analogous to superior fertility of soil; they are both monopolized natural agents; and the share which their owners obtain in the wealth which they contribute to produce is regulated by precisely the same principles. Men of genius, therefore, and country gentlemen, however little else they may have in common, yet being both proprietors of monopolized natural agents, would in an inquiry into the laws of wealth be properly placed in the same class. In the same way, the wages of a day laborer and the salary of a minister of state depend on the same principle—the demand for and supply of their services; and these persons, therefore, so widely different in their social position and importance, would be included by the economist in the same category. On the other hand, farmers and landlords, who, with a view to social inquiries, would probably be ranked together as belonging to the agricultural interest, would, if our object were the narrow one of the discovery of the laws of wealth, be properly placed in different classes: the income of the farmer depending on the laws which regulate the rate of profit, while that of the landlord depends on the laws which regulate rent; those laws being not only not the same, but generally varying in opposite directions.[1]

---

[1] Rent and profit possess under their superficial aspects so many attributes in common that it is not strange there should be a disposition to identify them as economic phenomena of the same kind. Among French economists in particular this view is nearly universal; not merely M. Say and those who have generally followed him, but that much abler thinker and clearer expositor, the late M. Cherbuliez, of Geneva, having so conceived the phenomena. It may be well, therefore, to set down briefly the facts which justify the distinction. 1. The rate of profit falls, that of rent rises, with the progress of society: the latter attains its maximum in old

As I have said, M. Say is one of those writers who have treated Political Economy as having this larger scope, and nowhere are the inconveniences of the method he pursues more distinctly brought into view than in his valuable treatise: indeed, it appears to me that most of the errors into which, notwithstanding the general merits of his work, he has fallen, are to be traced to this source. No one, I think, can peruse much of his writings without perceiving (and the same remark may be made of not a few French writers on Political Economy, and in particular of M. Bastiat) that his reasoning on economic problems is throughout carried on with a side glance at the prevalent socialistic doctrines. An inevitable consequence of this is—his object being quite as much to defend society and property against the attacks of their enemies as to elucidate the theory of wealth — that questions respecting the distribution of wealth are constantly confounded with the wholly different questions which the justification upon social grounds of existing institutions involves; and thus problems purely economic, come, under his treatment of

communities such as England, precisely where the former attains its minimum. 2. Rent and profit stand in different relations to price: *e. g.*, a rise of agricultural prices, if permanent, would imply, other things being the same, a rise of rent, but it would not imply or be attended with a rise of agricultural profits; on the contrary, agricultural profits, and profits generally, would most probably fall as a consequence of a rise in agricultural prices. 3. A tax on the profits of any particular branch of industry would raise prices in that industry; the receivers of profits would be thus enabled to transfer the burden of the tax to the consumers of the commodities they produce. A tax on rent would have no corresponding effect on agricultural prices and would rest definitively on the owners of the soil. 4. Variations in rents are slow, and, as a rule, in an upward direction; in profits, still more in interest, variations are frequent and rapid, and not in any constant direction.

them, to be complicated with considerations which are entirely foreign to their solution.

Thus he tells us[1] that rent, interest, and wages are all perfectly analogous : each giving the measure of utility which the productive agency (of which each respectively is the reward) subserves in production. Rent, according to this theory, does not depend on the different costs at which, owing to the physical qualities of the soil, agricultural produce is raised, nor profit on the cost of labor, nor wages on demand and supply,[2] but each on the utility of the functions which land, capital, and labor respectively perform in the creation of the ultimate product. Thus the distinct economic laws which regulate the distribution of wealth among the proprietors of these three productive agencies are confounded, in order to introduce a *moral* argument in defense of the existing structure of society, and to place the three classes of landlords, capitalists, and laborers on the same footing of social convenience and equity.

Dr. Whewell, in examining the cause of the failure of physical philosophy in the hands of the ancient Greeks, finds it in the circumstance that they introduced into their physical speculations ideas inappropriate to the facts which they endeavored to solve. It was not, he tells us, as is commonly supposed, that they undervalued the importance of facts ; for it appears that Aristotle collected facts in abundance ; nor yet that there was any dearth of ideas by which to generalize the facts

---

[1] "Cours Complet," tom. i. pp. 213–215.

[2] M. Say, it is true, in another part of his work (vol. ii. p. 45), states the law of wages correctly as depending on demand and supply, but the doctrine alluded to in the text is no less distinctly stated. The doctrines are, no doubt, irreconcilable ; but with this I am not concerned.

which they accumulated; but that, instead of steadily and exclusively fixing their attention on the purely physical ideas of force and pressure, they sought to account for external phenomena by resorting to moral considerations—to the ideas of strange and common, natural and unnatural, sympathy, horror, and the like—the result, of course, being that their inquiries led to nothing but fanciful theorizing and verbal quibbling.[1]

Now the introduction into economic discussions of such considerations as those to which I have adverted in the example given from M. Say appears to me to be an error of precisely the same kind as that which was committed by the ancient Greeks in their physical speculations, and one to which the method adopted by M. Say, of embracing in the same discussion the principles and ends of social union with the economic laws of wealth, seems almost inevitably to lead. The writer who thus treats Political Economy labors under a constant temptation to wander from those ideas which are strictly appropriate to his subject into considerations of equity and expediency which are proper only to the more extensive subject of society. Instead of addressing himself to the problem, according to what law certain facts result from certain principles, he proceeds to explain how the exist-

---

[1] Sir John Herschel's explanation of the failure is substantially the same. "Aristotle," he says, "at least saw the necessity of having recourse to nature for something like principles of physical science; and, as an observer, a collector, and a recorder of facts and phenomena, stood without an equal in his age. It was the fault of that age, and of the perverse and flimsy style of verbal disputation which had infected all learning, rather than his own, that he allowed himself to be contented with vague and loose notions drawn from general and vulgar observation, in place of seeking carefully, in well-arranged and thoroughly considered instances, for the laws of nature."

ence of the facts in question is consistent with social well-being and natural equity; and generally succeeds in deluding himself with the idea that he has solved an economic problem, when, in fact, he has only vindicated, or persuaded himself he has vindicated, a social arrangement.

The objections, therefore, to this method of treating Political Economy, resting as they do on the incompatible nature of the investigations which it seeks to combine, are fundamental. Even if it should be thought desirable to give the *name* of Political Economy to the larger inquiry, it would still be necessary to reserve for separate and distinct investigation the laws of the production and distribution of wealth.

§ 3. But, secondly, the ordinary definition represents Political Economy as a science; and (as I have elsewhere said) " for those who clearly apprehend what science, in the modern sense of the term, means, this ought sufficiently to indicate at once its province and what it undertakes to do. Unfortunately, many who perfectly understand what science means when the word is employed with reference to physical nature, allow themselves to slide into a totally different sense of it, or rather into acquiescence in an absence of all distinct meaning in its use, when they employ it with reference to social existence. In the minds of a large number of people every thing is Social Science which proposes to deal with social facts, either in the way of remedying a grievance, or in promoting order and progress in society: every thing is Political Economy which is in any way connected with the production, distribution, or consumption of wealth. Now I am anxious here to insist upon this fundamental point: whatever takes the form of a plan aiming at definite practical ends—it may be a measure for the diminution of pauperism, for the reform of land-tenure, for the extension of co-operative industry, for the regulation of the currency; or it may assume a more ambitious shape, and aim at reorganizing society under spiritual and temporal powers, represented by a high-priest of humanity and three bankers—it matters not what the proposal be, whether wide or narrow in its scope, severely judicious or wildly imprudent—if its object be to accomplish definite practical ends, then I say it has none of the characteristics of a science, and has no just claim to the name. Consider the case of any recognized physical science—Astronomy, Dynamics, Chemistry, Physiology—does any of these aim at definite practical ends? at modifying in a definite manner, it matters not how, the arrangement of things in the physical universe? Clearly not. In each case the object is, not to attain tangible results, not to prove any definite thesis, not to advocate any practical plan, but simply to give light, to reveal laws of nature, to tell us what phenomena are found together, what effects follow from what causes. Does it result from this that the physical sciences are without bearing on the practical concerns of mankind? I think I need not trouble myself to answer that question. Well, then, Political Economy is a science in the same sense in which Astronomy, Dynamics, Chemistry, Physiology are sciences. Its subject-matter is different; it deals with the phenomena of wealth, while they deal with the phenomena of the physical universe; but its methods, its aims, the character of its conclusions, are the same as theirs. What Astronomy does for the phenomena of the heavenly bodies; what Dynamics does for the phenomena of motion; what Chemistry does for the phenomena of chemical combination; what Physiology does for the phenomena of the functions of organic life, that Political Economy does for the phenomena of wealth: it expounds the laws according to which those phenomena co-exist with or succeed each other; that is to say, it expounds the laws of the phenomena of wealth.

"Let me here briefly explain what I mean by this expression. It is one in very frequent use; but, like many other expressions in frequent use, it does not always perhaps carry to the mind of the hearer a very definite idea. Of course I do not mean by the laws of the phenomena of wealth, Acts of Parliament. I mean the *natural* laws of those phenomena. Now what are the phenomena of wealth? Simply the facts of wealth; such facts as production, exchange, price; or, again, the various forms which wealth assumes in the process of distribution, such as wages, profits, rent, interest, and so forth. These are the phenomena of wealth; and the natural laws of these phenomena are certain constant relations in which they stand toward each other and toward their causes. For example, capital grows from year to year in England at a certain rate of progress; in the United States the rate is considerably more rapid; in China considerably slower. Now these facts are not fortuitous, but the natural result of causes; of such causes as the external physical circumstances of the countries in question, the intelligence and moral character of the people inhabiting them, and their political and social institutions; and so long as the causes remain the same, the results will remain the same. Similarly, the prices of commodities, the rent of land, the rates of wages, profits, and interest, differ in different countries; but here again, not at random. The particular forms which these phenomena assume are no more matters of chance than the temperature or the mineral productions of the countries in which they occur are matters of chance; or than the fauna or flora which flourish on the surface of those countries are matters of chance. Alike in the case of the physical and of the economic world, the facts we find existing are the results of causes, between which and them the connection is constant and invariable. It is, then, the constant relations exhibited in economic phenomena that we have in view when we speak of the laws of the phenomena of wealth; and in the exposition of these laws consists the science of Political Economy. If you ask me wherein lies the utility of such an exposition of economic laws, I answer, in precisely the same circumstance which constitutes the utility of all scientific knowledge. It teaches us the conditions of our power in relation to the facts of economic existence, the means by which, in the domain of material well-being, to attain our ends. It is by such knowledge that man becomes the minister and interpreter of Nature, and learns to control Nature by obeying her.

"And now I beg you to observe what follows from this mode of conceiving our study. In the first place, then, you will remark that, as thus conceived, Political Economy stands apart from all particular systems of social or industrial existence. It has nothing to do with *laissez-faire* any more than with communism; with freedom of contract any more than with paternal government, or with systems of *status*. It stands apart from all particular systems, and is, moreover, absolutely neutral as between all. Not of course that the knowledge which it gives may not be employed to recommend some and to discredit others. This is inevitable, and is only the proper and legitimate use of economic knowledge. But this notwithstanding, the science is neutral, as between social schemes, in this important sense. It pronounces no judgment on the worthiness or desirableness of the ends aimed at in such systems. It tells us what their effects will be as regards a specific class of facts, thus contributing *data* toward the formation of a sound opinion respecting them. But here its function ends. The data thus furnished may indeed go far to determine our judgment, but they do not necessarily, and should not in practice always, do so. For there are few practical problems which do not present other aspects than the purely economical—political, moral, educational, artistic aspects —and these may involve consequences so weighty as to turn the scale against purely economic solutions. On the relative importance of such conflicting considerations Political Economy offers no opinion, pronounces no judgment—thus, as I said, standing neutral between competing social schemes; neutral, as the science of Mechanics stands neutral between competing plans of railway construction, in which expense, for instance, as well as mechanical efficiency, is to be considered; neutral, as Chemistry stands neutral between competing plans of sanitary improvement; as Physiology stands neutral between opposing systems of medicine. It supplies the means, or, more correctly, a portion of

the means for estimating all; it refuses to identify
itself with any.

"Now I desire to call particular attention to this characteristic of economic science, because I do not think it
is at all generally appreciated, and because some serious
and indeed lamentable consequences have arisen from
overlooking it.   For example, it is sometimes supposed
that because Political Economy comprises in its expositions theories of wages, profits, and rent, the science is
therefore committed to the approval of our present mode
of industrial life, under which three distinct classes—laborers, capitalists, and landlords—receive remuneration in
those forms.   Under this impression, some social reform-
ers, whose ideal of industrial life involves a modification
of our existing system, have thought themselves called
upon to denounce and deride economic science, as forsooth seeking to stereotype the existing forms of industrial life, and of course therefore opposed to their views.
But this is a complete mistake.   Economic science has
no more connection with our present industrial system
than the science of mechanics has with our present system
of railways.   Our existing railway lines have been laid
down according to the best extant mechanical knowledge; but we do not think it necessary on this account,
as a preliminary to improving our railways, to denounce
mechanical science.   If wages, profits, and rent find a
place in economic theories, this is simply because these
are the forms which the distribution of wealth assumes
as society is now constituted.   They are phenomena which
need to be explained.   But it comes equally within the
province of the economist to exhibit the working of any
proposed modification of this system, and to set forth the

operation of the laws of production and distribution under such new conditions.

" And, in connection with this point, I may make this remark : that, so far is it from being true, as some would seem to suppose, that economic science has done its work, and thus become obsolete for practical purposes, an object of mere historical curiosity, it belongs, on the contrary, to a class of sciences whose work can never be completed, never at least so long as human beings continue to progress; for the most important portion of the data from which it reasons is human character and human institutions, and every thing consequently which affects that character or those institutions must create new problems for economic science. Unlike the physicist, who deals with phenomena incapable of development, always essentially the same, the main facts of the economist's study—man as an industrial being, man as organized in society—are ever undergoing change. The economic conditions of patriarchal life, of Greek or Roman life, of feudal life, are not the economic conditions of modern commercial life; and had Political Economy been cultivated in those primitive, ancient, or mediæval times, while it would doubtless have contained some expositions which we do not now find in it, it must also have wanted many which it now contains. One has only to turn to the discussions on currency and credit which have accompanied the great development of England's commerce during the last half-century to see how the changing needs of an advancing society evolve new problems for the economist, and call forth new growths of economic doctrine. At this moment one may see that such an occasion is imminent. Since the economic doctrines now holding their place in English text-books were thought out, a new mode of industrial organization has established itself in Great Britain and other countries. Co-operation is now a reality, and, if the signs are not all deceptive, bids fair to transform much of England's industry. Now the characteristic feature of co-operation, looked at from the economic point of view, is that it combines in the same person the two capacities of laborer and capitalist; whereas our present theories of industrial remuneration presuppose a division of those capacities between distinct persons. Obviously, our existing theories must fail to elucidate a state of things different from that contemplated in their elaboration. We have thus need of a new exposition of the law of industrial remuneration—an exposition suited to a state of things in which the gains of producers, instead of taking the form of wages, profits, and rent, are realized in a single composite sum. · I give this as an example of the new developments of economic theory which the progress of society will constantly call for. Of course it is an open question whether this *is* the direction in which industrial society is moving; and there are those, I know, who hold that it is not toward co-operation, but rather toward 'captains of industry' and organization of workmen on the military plan, that the current is setting. It may be so, and in this case the economic problem of the future will not be that which I have suggested above; nevertheless, *an* economic problem there still will be. If society were organized tomorrow on the principles of M. Comte, so long as physical and human nature remain what they are, the phenomena of wealth would exhibit constant relations, would still be governed by natural laws; and those relations, those laws, it would still be important to know. The function of the economist would be as needful as ever.

"A far more serious consequence, however, of ignoring the neutral attitude of this study in relation to questions of practical reform is the effect it has had in alienating from it the minds of the working classes. Instead of appearing in the neutral guise of an expositor of truths, the contributor of certain data toward the solution of social problems—data which of themselves commit no man to any course, and of which the practical cogency can only be determined after all the other data implicated in the problem are known—instead of presenting itself as Chemistry, Physiology, Mechanics present themselves, Political Economy too often makes its appearance, especially in its approaches to the working classes, in the guise of a dogmatic code of cut-and-dried rules, a system promulgating decrees, 'sanctioning' one social arrangement, 'condemning' another, requiring from men, not consideration, but obedience. Now when we take into account the sort of decrees which are ordinarily given to the world in the name of Political Economy—decrees which I think I may say in the main amount to a handsome ratification of the existing form of society as approximately perfect—I think we shall be able to understand the repugnance, and even violent opposition, manifested toward it by people who have their own reasons for not cherishing that unbounded admiration for our present industrial arrangements which is felt by some popular expositors of so-called economic laws. When a working man is told that Political Economy 'condemns' strikes, hesitates about co-operation, looks askance at proposals for limiting the hours of labor, but 'approves' the accumulation of capital, and 'sanctions' the market rate of wages, it seems not an unnatural response that 'since Political Economy is against the working man, it behooves the working man to be against Political Economy.' It seems not unnatural that this new code should come to be regarded with suspicion, as a system possibly contrived in the interest of employers, which it is the workmen's wisdom simply to repudiate and disown. Economic science is thus placed in an essentially false position, and the section of the community which is most vitally interested in taking to heart its truths is effectually prevented from even giving them a hearing. I think it, therefore, a matter not merely of theoretic but of the utmost practical importance, that the strictly scientific character of this study should be insisted upon. It is only when so presented that its true position in relation to practical reforms, and its really benevolent bearing toward all sorts and conditions of men, will be understood, and that we can hope to overcome those deep-seated but perfectly natural prejudices with which the most numerous class in the community unfortunately regard it." [1]

---

[1] "Essays in Political Economy, Theoretical and Applied," pp. 252-261.

LECTURE II.

OF THE MENTAL AND PHYSICAL PREMISES OF PO-
LITICAL ECONOMY, AND OF THE LOGICAL
CHARACTER OF THE DOCTRINES
THENCE DEDUCED.

§ 1. In my last lecture I called attention to the conception of Political Economy formed by the leading writers on the subject in England, and in particular I took occasion to point out the significance of the words which describe it as the "Science of Wealth." We have now reached a point at which it may be well to attempt some more precise determination of its character and scope, and, with a view to this, to consider the position occupied by economic speculation in relation to the two great departments of existence—matter and mind. With regard to this aspect of the case, the following theory has been advanced by high authorities:

"In all the intercourse of man with nature, whether we consider him as acting upon it, or as receiving impressions from it, the effect or phenomenon depends upon causes of two kinds: the properties of the object acting, and those of the object acted upon. Every thing which can possibly happen, in which man and external things are jointly concerned, results from the joint operation of a law or laws of matter and a law or laws of the human mind. Thus the production of corn by human labor is the result of a law of mind and many laws of matter. The laws of matter are those properties of the soil and of vegetable life which cause the seed to germinate in the ground, and those properties of the human body which render food necessary to its support. The law of mind is that man desires to possess subsistence, and consequently wills the necessary means of procuring it. Laws of mind and laws of matter are so dissimilar in their nature that it would be contrary to all principles of rational arrangement to mix them up as part of the same study. In all scientific methods, therefore, they are placed apart. Any compound effect or phenomenon which depends both on the properties of matter and on those of mind may thus become the subject of two completely distinct sciences, or branches of science: one treating of the phenomenon in so far as it depends upon the laws of matter only; the other treating of it in so far as it depends upon the laws of mind.

"The physical sciences are those which treat of the laws of matter, and of all complex phenomena, in so far as dependent upon the laws of matter. The mental or moral sciences are those which treat of the laws of mind, and of all complex phenomena, in so far as dependent upon the laws of mind. Most of the moral sciences presuppose physical science; but few of the physical sciences presuppose moral science. The reason is obvious. There are many phenomena (an earthquake, for example, or the motions of the planets) which depend upon the laws of matter exclusively, and have nothing whatever to do with the laws of mind. Many of the physical sciences may be treated of without any reference to mind, and as if the mind existed as a recipient of knowledge only, not as a cause producing effects. But there are no phenomena which depend *exclusively* upon the laws of mind; even the phenomena of the mind itself being partially dependent upon the physiological laws of the body. All the mental sciences, therefore, not excepting the pure science of mind, must take account of a great variety of physical truths; and (as physical science is commonly and very properly studied first) may be said to presuppose them, taking up the complex phenomena where physical science leaves them.

"Now this, it will be found, is a precise statement of the relation in which Political Economy stands to the various sciences which are tributary to the arts of production.

"The laws of the production of the objects which constitute wealth are the subject-matter both of Political Economy and of almost all the physical sciences. Such, however, of those laws as are purely laws of matter belong to physical science, and that exclusively. Such of them as are laws of the human mind, and no others, belong to Political Economy, which finally sums up the result of both combined." [1]

The view here set forth has been accepted by another high authority, Mr. Senior, who, in an article in the *Edinburgh Review* (Oct., 1848), comments as follows upon the passage just quoted:

"The justice of these views, we think, is obvious; and, though they are now for the first time formally stated, an indistinct perception of them must be general, since they are generally acted on. The Political Economist does not attempt to state the mechanical and chemical laws which enable the steam-engine to perform its miracles. He passes them by as laws of matter; but he explains as fully as his knowledge will allow the motives which induce the mechanist to erect the steam-engine and the laborer to work it: and these are laws of mind. He leaves to the geologist to explain the laws of matter which occasion the formation of coal; to the chemist, to distinguish its component elements; to the engineer, to state the means by which it is extracted; and to the teachers of many hundred different arts to point out the uses to which it may be applied. What he reserves to himself is to explain the laws

---

[1] "Essays on some Unsettled Questions in Political Economy," by J. S. Mill, pp. 130–132.

of mind under which the owner of the soil allows his past-
ures to be laid waste, and the minerals which they cover
to be abstracted; under which the capitalist employs in
sinking shafts and piercing galleries funds which might
be devoted to his own immediate enjoyment; under which
the miner encounters the toils and the dangers of his haz-
ardous and laborious occupation; and the laws, also laws
of mind, which decide in what proportions the produce or
the value of the produce is divided between the three
classes by whose concurrence it has been obtained. When
he uses as his premises, as he often must do, facts supplied
by physical science, he does not attempt to account for
them."

The concluding sentence in the passage taken from
Mr. Mill's Essay, in which he says that Political Economy "finally sums up the result of both [laws of mind
and of matter] combined," seems to me to describe correctly the function of the science, but to be inconsistent
with the tenor of the remarks which precede it, as it is
plainly inconsistent with Mr. Senior's interpretation of
the passage. Excluding that sentence, the effect of the exposition is that Political Economy belongs to the group
of sciences "which treats of the laws of mind, and of
all complex phenomena, in so far as dependent upon the
laws of mind," and is, therefore, properly described as a
"mental" or "moral" science; while its relation to the
world of matter being of a different and altogether less
intimate character, it is properly kept apart from the
physical group. The facts and laws of material nature
it takes for granted; but the facts and laws of mind, so
far as these are involved in the production and distribution of wealth, constitute its proper province, furnishing
the phenomena of which it "treats" and which it "ex-

plains." To this effect, it seems to me, is the view fairly deducible from the passages I have quoted; and, so far as I know, the doctrine, as I have stated it, has been generally acquiesced in by later writers. Now from this view of the character of Political Economy I venture to dissent. It appears to me that the laws and phenomena of wealth which it belongs to this science to explain depend equally on physical and on mental laws; that Political Economy stands in precisely the same relation to physical and to mental nature; and that, if it is to be ranked in either of these departments of speculation, it is as well entitled to be placed in the one as in the other.

The expressions "physical" and "mental," as applied to science, have generally been employed to designate those branches of knowledge of which physical and mental phenomena respectively form the subject-matter. Thus Chemistry is considered as a physical science because the subject-matter on which chemical inquiry is exercised, viz., material elements and combinations, is physical. Psychology, on the other hand, is a mental science; the subject-matter of it being mental states and feelings. And as the office of the chemist consists in observing and analyzing material objects with a view to discovering the laws of their elementary constitution, so that of the psychologist consists in endeavoring, by means of reflection on what passes in his own, or appears to pass in the minds of others, to ascertain the laws by which the phenomena of our mental constitution succeed and produce each other. If this be a correct statement of the principle on which the designations "mental" and "physical" are applied to the sciences, it seems to follow that Political Economy does not find a place under either category. Neither mental nor physical nature forms the *subject-matter* of the investigations of the political economist. He considers, it is true, physical phenomena, as he also considers mental phenomena, but in neither case as phenomena which it belongs to his science to explain. The subject-matter of that science is wealth; and though wealth consists in material objects, it is not wealth in virtue of those objects being material, but in virtue of their possessing value—that is to say, in virtue of their possessing a quality attributed to them by the mind. The subject-matter of Political Economy is thus neither purely physical nor purely mental, but possesses a complex character, equally derived from both departments of nature, and the laws of which are neither mental nor physical laws, though they are dependent, and, as I maintain, dependent equally on the laws of matter and on those of mind.

Let us consider, for example, the causes which determine the rate of wages. This, it will be admitted on all hands, is an economic problem. It is evident that the objects which the laborer receives are material objects, but those material objects are invested by the mind with a peculiar attribute in consequence of which they are considered as possessing value; and it is in their complex character, as physical objects invested with the attribute of value, that the political economist considers them. The subject-matter, therefore, of the wages-problem possesses qualities derived alike from physical and from mental nature; consequently, if it is to be denominated from the nature of its subject-matter, it is equally entitled or disentitled to the character of a physical or mental problem.

But it is said that Political Economy considers the problem no further than as it depends on the action of the human mind. The food and clothing which the laborer consumes have, no doubt, physical properties, as the laborer himself has a physical as well as a mental nature; but with the physical properties, we are told, the political economist has no concern: he considers those objects so far forth only as they possess value, and value is a purely mental conception. But is this true? Does the political economist — does Mr. Senior, *e. g.*, in his purely scientific treatment of this question—entirely put out of consideration the physical properties of the commodities which the laborer consumes, or the physiological conditions on which the increase of the laboring population depends? What is the solution of the wages-problem? Wages, it will be said, depend on demand and supply; or, more explicitly, on the relation between the amount of capital applied to the payment of wages and the number of laborers seeking employment. But the amount of capital employed in the payment of wages depends, among other causes, on the productiveness of industry in raising the commodities of the laborer's consumption—a circumstance which is equally dependent on the laws of physical nature and on the mental qualities which the workman brings to his task. The number of laborers seeking employment, again, depends, among other causes, on the laws of population; while these are determined as much by the physiological laws of the body as the psychological laws of the mind, the political economist taking equal cognizance of both.

It thus appears that as the subject-matter of Political Economy, viz., wealth, possesses qualities derived equally

C

from the world of matter and from that of mind, so its premises are equally drawn from both these departments of nature. The latter point, indeed, is admitted by the authorities to whom I have referred, who, nevertheless, by what I must deem a strange oversight, represent the science as investigating the laws of wealth no further than as they depend on the laws of the human mind.

But perhaps this point will be made more clear—the equal dependence, namely, of the science of Political Economy on the laws of the physical world and on those of the human mind—if we consider that a change in the character of the former laws will equally affect its conclusions with a change in that of the latter. The physical qualities of the soil, *e. g.*, under the present constitution of nature, are such that, after a certain quantum of cultivation has been applied to a limited area, a further application is not attended with a proportionate return. The proof of this is that, instead of confining cultivation to the best soils, and forcing them to yield the whole amount of food that may be required, it is found profitable to resort to soils of inferior quality.[1]

---

[1] This doctrine has been denied, and some curious arguments have been advanced in refutation of it. The topic most insisted on by those who controvert it is the superior productiveness of agricultural industry in the United Kingdom *at present*, as compared with that which prevailed in former periods, notwithstanding the greater amount of capital now employed in agriculture. This argument would be good for something if all the other conditions of the problem were the same; but it is certain that they are not the same, and that they differ precisely in the point that is of importance—the superior skill with which capital and industry are at present applied. No economist that I am aware of has ever said that a small and unskillful application of capital to land would necessarily be attended with greater proportional returns than a larger outlay more skillfully applied; and it is to this assertion only that the argument in question applies.

This physical fact, as every political economist knows, and as shall be explained on a future occasion, leads, through the play of human desires in the pursuit of wealth, to the phenomenon of rent, to the fall of profits as communities advance, and to a retardation in the ad-

---

But it is important to remark that the attempt to meet the doctrine in question by statistical data implies (as will hereafter more clearly appear) a total misconception, both of the fact which is asserted and of the *kind* of proof which an economic doctrine requires. The doctrine contains, not a historic generalization to be tested by documentary evidence, but a statement as to an existing physical fact, which, if seriously questioned, can only be conclusively determined by actual experiment upon the existing soil. If any one denies the fact, it is open to him to refute it by making the experiment. Let him show that he can obtain from a limited area of soil any required quantity of produce by simply increasing the outlay—that is to say, that by quadrupling or decupling the outlay he can obtain a quadruple or decuple return. If it be asked why those who maintain the affirmative of the doctrine do not establish their view by actual experiment, the answer is that the experiment is performed for them by every practical farmer; and that the fact of the diminishing productiveness of the soil is proved by their conduct in preferring to resort to inferior soils rather than force unprofitably soils of better quality.

Mr. Carey, the American economist, has endeavored to meet this reasoning by urging that the conduct of farmers in resorting to inferior soils after the better qualities have been all taken into cultivation, no more constitutes a proof that industry on the superior soils has become less productive than the conduct of a cotton-spinner in building a second factory when his first is full is a proof that manufacturing industry tends to become less productive as manufacturing capital and labor increase. This is, in other words, to say that the reason farmers do not increase their outlay on the soils of superior quality is, not because it would be unprofitable to do so, but for the same reason which limits the amount of capital and the number of hands employed in a cotton-mill, namely, that the necessary conditions of space being taken into account, it would *be impossible to do so.* No one who holds the received theory of rent will hesitate to stake the doctrine upon the issue. When any sane farmer in the United Kingdom, or in any other quarter of the civilized world, will give the same answer to the question, "Why he does not manure more highly, or drain more deeply, or plow more frequently, a given field?" which Mr. Carey gives, viz., "want of room," the disciples of Ricardo will be prepared to abandon their master; but *till* this specimen of bucolic exegesis is produced they will probably retain their present views.

vance of population. If the fact were otherwise—if the
physical properties of the soil were such as to admit of
an indefinite increase of produce in undiminished proportion to the outlay by simply increasing the outlay—
if, *e. g.*, it were found that by doubling the quantity of
manure upon a given acre and by plowing it twice as
often, a farmer could obtain a double produce, and by a
quadruple outlay a quadruple produce, and so on *ad in-
finitum;* if this were so, the science of Political Economy, as it at present exists, would be as completely
revolutionized as if human nature itself were altered—
as if benevolence, for example, were so strengthened at
the expense of self-love that human beings should refuse
to avail themselves, at the expense of their neighbors, of
those special advantages with which nature or fortune
may happen to endow them; under such a change in the
physical qualities of the soil rent would disappear, profits
would have no tendency permanently to fall, and population in the oldest countries might advance as rapidly
as in the newest colonies.

I am, therefore, disposed to regard Political Economy
as belonging neither to the department of physical nor
to that of mental inquiry, but as occupying an intermediate position, and as referable to the class of studies
which includes historical, political, and, in general, social
investigations. The class appears to me to be a class *sui
generis*, having for its subject-matter the complex phenomena presented by the concurrence of physical, physiological, and mental laws, and for its function the tracing of such phenomena to their physical, physiological,
and mental causes.

Thus, to take an example from Political Economy, rent

is a complex phenomenon, arising (as has been already intimated) from the play of human interests when brought into contact with the actual physical conditions of the soil in relation to the physiological character of vegetable productions. If these physical conditions were different, if capital and labor could be applied to a limited portion of the soil indefinitely with undiminished return, a small portion only of the best land in the country would be cultivated, and no farmer would consent to pay rent; on the other hand, if the principle of self-interest were absent, no landlord would exact it. Both conditions are indispensable, and equally indispensable, to the existence of rent: they are the premises from which the theory is deduced. It is for the political economist to prove, first, that the premises are true in fact; and, secondly, that they account for the phenomenon; but when this is done, his business is ended. He does not attempt to explain the physical laws on which the qualities of the soil depend; and no more does he undertake to analyze the nature of those feelings of self-interest in the minds of the landlord and tenant which regulate the terms of the bargain. He regards them both as facts, not to be analyzed and explained, but to be ascertained and taken account of; not as the subject-matter, but as the basis of his reasonings. If further information be desired, recourse must be had to other sciences: the physical fact he hands over to the chemist or the physiologist; the mental to the psychological or the ethical scholar.

In the considerations just adduced, we may perceive what the proper limits are of economic inquiry—at what point the economist, in tracing the phenomena of wealth to their causes and laws, may properly stop and consider his task as completed, his problem as solved. It is precisely at that point at which in the course of his reasonings he finds himself in contact with some phenomenon *not* economic, with some physical or mental fact, some political or social institution. So soon as he has traced the phenomena of wealth to causes of this order, he has reached the proper goal of his researches; and such causes, therefore, are properly regarded as "ultimate" in relation to economic science. Not that they may not deserve and admit of further analysis and explanation, but that this analysis and explanation is not the business of the economist—is not the specific problem which he undertakes to solve.[1]

The position of Political Economy, as just described, may be illustrated by that of Geology in relation to the sciences of Mechanics, Chemistry, and Physiology. The complex phenomena presented by the constitution of the earth's crust form the subject-matter of the science of the geologist; they are the complex result of mechanical, chemical, and physiological laws, and the business of the geologist is to trace them to these causes; but having done this, his labors as a geologist are at an end: the further investigation of the problem belongs not to Geology, but to Mechanics, Chemistry, and Physiology.

§ 2. The premises, or ultimate facts, of Political Economy being thus drawn alike from the world of matter and from that of mind, it remains that I should indicate the character of those facts, physical and mental, from which the conclusions of the science are derived; in

---

[1] Appendix B.

other words, that I should show in what manner the facts which are pertinent to economic investigations are to be distinguished from those which are not. The answer to this question must in general be determined by considering what the science proposes to accomplish. This, as you are aware, is the discovery of the laws of the production and distribution of wealth. The facts, therefore, which constitute the premises of Political Economy are those which influence the production and distribution of wealth; and in order that the science be absolutely perfect, so that an economist might predict the course of economic phenomena with the same accuracy and certainty with which an astronomer predicts the course of celestial phenomena, it would be necessary that these premises should include every fact, mental and physical, which influences the phenomena of wealth.

It does not, however, seem possible that this degree of perfection should ever be attained. In Political Economy, as in all those branches of inquiry which include among their premises at once the moral and physical nature of man, the facts to be taken account of are so numerous, their character so various, and the laws of their sequence so obscure, that it would seem scarcely possible to ascertain them all, much less to assign to each its exact value. And even if this were possible, the task of tracing these principles to their consequences, allowing to each its due significance, and no more than its due significance, would present a problem so complex and difficult as to defy the powers of the most accomplished reasoners.

But although this is so, and although, therefore, neither Political Economy nor any of the class of inquiries to

which it belongs may ever be expected to reach that
perfection which has been attained in some of the more
advanced physical sciences, yet this does not forbid us to
hope that, by following in our economic investigations
the same course which has been pursued with such success in physical science, we may attain, if not to absolute
scientific perfection, at least to the discovery of solid and
valuable results.

The desires, passions, and propensities which influence
mankind in the pursuit of wealth are, as I have intimated, almost infinite; yet among these there are some
principles of so marked and paramount a character as
both to admit of being ascertained, and, when ascertained,
to afford the data for determining the most important
laws of the production and distribution of wealth, in so
far as these laws are affected by mental causes.   To possess himself of these is the first business of the political
economist; he has then to take account of some leading
physiological facts connected with human nature; and,
lastly, to ascertain the principal physical characteristics
of those natural agents of production on which human
industry is exercised.   Thus he will consider, as being
included among the paramount mental principles to
which I have alluded, the general desire for physical
well-being, and for wealth as the means of obtaining it;
the intellectual power of judging of the efficacy of means
to an end, along with the inclination to reach our ends
by the easiest and shortest means—mental facts from
which results the desire to obtain wealth at the least possible sacrifice; he will further duly weigh those propensities which, in conjunction with the physiological conditions of the human frame, determine the laws of popu-

lation; and, lastly, he will take into account the physical qualities of the soil, and of those other natural agents on which the labor and ingenuity of man are employed. These facts, whether mental or physical, he will consider, as I have already stated, not with a view to explain them, but as the data of his reasoning, as leading causes affecting the production and distribution of wealth.

But it must not be thought that, when these cardinal facts have been ascertained and their consequences duly developed, the labors of the political economist are at an end, even supposing that his treatment of them has been exhaustive and his reasoning without a flaw. Though the conclusions thus arrived at will, in the main, correspond with the actual course of events, yet great and glaring discrepancies will frequently occur. The data on which his speculations have been based include, indeed, the grand and leading causes which regulate the production and distribution of wealth, but they do not include all the causes. Many subordinate influences (subordinate, I mean, in relation to the ends of Political Economy) will intervene to disturb, and occasionally to reverse, the operation of the more powerful principles, and thus to modify the resulting phenomena. The next step, therefore, in his investigations will be to endeavor as far as possible to ascertain the character of those subordinate causes, whether physical or mental, political or social, which influence human conduct in the pursuit of wealth; and these, when he has found them and is enabled to appreciate them with sufficient accuracy, he will incorporate among the premises of the science, as data to be taken account of in his future speculations.

Thus the political and social institutions of a country, and in particular the laws affecting the tenure of land, will be included among such subordinate agencies; and it will be for the political economist to show in what way causes of this kind modify the operation of more fundamental principles in relation to the phenomena which it belongs to his science to investigate.

Again, any great discovery in the arts of production, such, *e. g.*, as the steam-engine, will be a new fact for the consideration of the political economist; it will be for him to consider its effect on the productiveness of industry or the distribution of its products; how far and in what directions it is calculated to affect wages, profits, and rent, and to modify those conclusions to which he may have been led by reasoning from the state of productive industry previous to its introduction. It will be like the discovery to an astronomer of a new planet, the attraction of which, operating on all the heavenly bodies within the sphere of its influence, will cause them more or less to deviate from the path which had been previously calculated for them. It is a new force, which, in speculating on the tendencies of economic phenomena, the political economist will include as a new datum among his premises.

In the same way, also, those motives and principles of action which may be developed in the progress of society—so far as they may be found to affect the phenomena of wealth—will also be taken account of by the political economist. He will consider, *e. g.*, the influence of custom in modifying human conduct in the pursuit of wealth; he will consider how, as civilization advances, the estimation of the future in relation to the present is enhanced, and the desire for immediate enjoyment is controlled by the increasing efficacy of prudential restraint; he will also observe how ideas of decency, comfort, and luxury are developed as society progresses, modifying the natural force of the principles of population, influencing the mode of expenditure of different classes, and affecting thereby the distribution of industrial products.

The question is sometimes asked—How far should moral and religious considerations be admitted as coming within the purview of Political Economy?[1] and the doctrine now under exposition enables us to supply the answer. Moral and religious considerations are to be taken account of by the economist precisely in so far as they are found, in fact, to affect the conduct of men in the pursuit of wealth. In so far as they operate in this way, such considerations are as pertinent to his inquiries as the desire for physical well-being, or the propensity in human beings to reproduce their kind; and they are only less important as premises of his science than the latter principles, because they are far less influential with regard to the phenomena which constitute the subject-matter of his inquiries.

As I have already remarked, it is scarcely possible that all these circumstances should be ascertained or accurately appreciated; but it seems quite possible that some of the most important of them may, with sufficient accuracy at least to be made available as data for subsequent deductions, and be entitled to a place among the premises of the science. And in proportion as this

---

[1] To be distinguished from another question with which it is commonly confounded, viz., How far should economic considerations be made subordinate to considerations of morality in the art of government?

is done, in proportion to the completeness of its premises, and to the skill with which they are reasoned upon, will the science of Political Economy approximate toward that perfection which has been attained in other branches of knowledge; in the same degree will its conclusions correspond with actual events, and its doctrines become safe and trustworthy guides to the practical statesman and the philanthropist.

§ 3. Having now considered the character and limits of Political Economy, I shall conclude this lecture by adverting briefly to a point—not, as might at first sight seem, of purely theoretic importance—on which some high authorities are at variance. I allude to the question whether Political Economy be a positive or a hypothetical science.

It does not appear that the meaning of the terms " positive " and " hypothetical," as they have been used in this controversy, has been precisely fixed, and I am disposed to think that the difference of opinion which prevails may, in a great measure, be resolved into an ambiguity of language. Let us consider, then, what is to be understood by the terms " positive " and " hypothetical " when applied to a science.

In the first place, we may describe a science as " positive " or " hypothetical " with reference to the character of its premises. It is in this sense that we speak of Mathematics as a hypothetical science, its premises being arbitrary conceptions framed by the mind, which have nothing corresponding to them in the world of real existence; and it is in this sense that we distinguish it from the positive physical sciences, the premises of which are laid in the existing facts of nature. But "positive" and "hypothetical" may also be used with reference to the conclusions of a science; and in this sense all the physical sciences which have advanced so far as to admit of deductive reasoning must be considered hypothetical, in contradistinction to those less advanced sciences which, being still in the purely inductive stage, express in their conclusions merely observed and generalized facts. The conclusions, *e. g.*, of a mechanician or of an astronomer, though correctly deduced from premises representing concrete realities, may have nothing accurately to correspond with them in nature. The mechanician may have overlooked the disturbing influence of friction. The astronomer may have been ignorant of the existence of some planet, the attractive force of which may be an essential element in the solution of his problem. The conclusions of each, therefore, when applied to facts, can only be said to be true *in the absence of disturbing causes;* which is, in other words, to say that they are true on *the hypothesis* that the premises include all the causes affecting the result. The correspondence of such deductions with facts may, according to the circumstances of each case, possess any degree of probability, from a mere presumption in favor of a particular result to a probability scarcely distinguishable from absolute certainty. This will depend on the degree of perfection which the science has attained; but, whatever be that degree of perfection, from the limited nature of man's faculties he can never be sure that he is in possession of all the premises affecting the result, and therefore can never be certain that his conclusions represent positive realities. Speaking, therefore, with reference to the conclusions of those physical sciences in which deductive reasoning is employed, such sciences must be regarded as hypothetical.

On the other hand, in those sciences which have not advanced far enough to admit of deductive reasoning, such laws as they have arrived at, being mere generalized statements of observed phenomena, represent not hypothetical but positive truth. Such are the generalized facts in geology and in many of the natural sciences.

Now Political Economy seems in this respect plainly to belong to the same class of sciences with Mechanics, Astronomy, Optics, Chemistry, Electricity, and, in general, all those physical sciences which have reached the deductive stage. Its premises are not arbitrary figments of the mind, formed without reference to concrete existences, like those of Mathematics ; nor are its conclusions mere generalized statements of observed facts, like those of the purely inductive natural sciences. But, like Mechanics or Astronomy, its premises represent positive facts ; while its conclusions, like the conclusions of these sciences, may or may not correspond to the realities of external nature, and therefore must be considered as representing only hypothetical truth.

It is positively true, *e. g.*, to assert that men desire wealth, that they seek, according to their lights, the easiest and shortest means by which to attain their ends, and that consequently they desire to obtain wealth with the least exertion of labor possible ; and it is a logical deduction from this principle that, where perfect liberty of action is permitted, laborers will seek those employments, and capitalists those modes of investing their capital, in which, *ceteris paribus,* wages and profits are highest. It is further a necessary consequence of this principle that, were it universally and constantly acted upon, the rate of profit and the rate of wages over the whole world would not indeed be the same, but would stand, or tend to stand, in the same relation to the actual sacrifices undergone by the recipients of these two kinds of remuneration. Yet so far is this from being the case that there are scarcely two countries in which wages and profits (meaning thereby the average rate of each) are not permanently different. The French laborer will content himself with the rate of wages which prevails in France, rather than cross the Atlantic for a double remuneration. The English capitalist will prefer eight or ten per cent. profit with English society to the quadruple returns of California or Australia. The same inequality which we find in the average rates of wages and profits prevailing in different countries we find also in a less degree in the different departments of productive industry in the same country. What in the former case is done by the love of country to control the simple desire for wealth and aversion to labor, and to modify the resulting phenomena, is done in the latter by the ignorance and poverty of large classes which disable them for competing for the more lucrative employments, and by opinions and prejudices respecting the degree of credit or respectability attaching to particular trades and employments, such as prevail in every civilized community.

It is evident, therefore, that an economist, arguing from the unquestionable facts of man's nature—the desire of wealth and the aversion to labor—and arguing

with strict logical accuracy, may yet, if he omit to notice other principles also affecting the question, be land-
ed in conclusions which have no resemblance to existing realities. But he can never be certain that he does
not omit some essential circumstance, and, indeed, it is
scarcely possible to include all : it is evident, therefore,
that, as is the case in those deductive physical sciences
to which I have alluded, his conclusions will correspond
with facts *only in the absence of disturbing causes*,
which is, in other words, to say that they represent not
positive but hypothetic truth.[1]

It thus appears that Political Economy, according as
we consider it with reference to its premises or to the
doctrines deduced from them, must be regarded in the
one case as a positive, in the other as a hypothetical science. It is, however, to be remarked that that portion
of the science which represents positive truth—its prem-

---

[1] In entire accord with this is M. A. E. Cherbuliez in his admirable
" Précis de la Science Économique :"

" Qu'est-ce qu'une vérité scientifique ? C'est l'expression d'une idée,
ou d'une loi générale, à laquelle notre intelligence arrive en partant de
certaines données fournies par l'observation immédiate. Nous analysons
un certain nombre de phénomènes pour en tirer ce qu'ils ont de commun ;
puis nous raisonnons d'après ces résultats de l'analyse, pour construire
une théorie scientifique. Si nous avons bien observé, si notre raisonne-
ment a été correct, la conséquence est aussi vraie que la donnée générale
d'où elle découle, mais elle ne peut l'être davantage, ni d'une autre ma-
nière. Or, la donnée générale n'est pas une réalité ; elle n'est qu'une ab-
straction, au moins dans la plupart des cas. Pour l'obtenir, qu'avons-
nous fait ? Nous avons dépouillé les phénomènes réels de ce qui les
rendait complexes et divers, pour ne voir que ce qu'ils avaient de commun. Le résultat de cette analyse peut donc fort bien ne représenter
rien de réel, ne ressembler exactement à aucun des phénomènes complexes de la réalité. Des lors, la théorie la loi, que nous construisons
d'après ce résultat, peut aussi ne se vérifier dans aucun des faits que nous
verrons s'accomplir sous nos yeux. Cette théorie, cette loi n'en sera pas
moins une vérité scientifique."—Tome I. pp. 10, 11.

ises, namely, or the facts, mental and physical, upon which it rests — belongs to it in common with many other sciences and arts. All that is properly speaking Political Economy is that system of doctrines which has been or may be deduced from those premises ; and all this represents, as I have shown, hypothetical truth. It appears to me, therefore, clearly proper that Political Economy should be classed as a hypothetical science.

But in thus describing Political Economy, I have ventured to dissent from the high authority of Mr. Senior. I shall, therefore, read you the passage in which he expresses his objections to regarding Political Economy as a hypothetical science :

"The hypothetical treatment of the science appears to me to be open to three great objections. In the first place, it is obviously unattractive. No one listens to an exposition of what might be the state of things under given but unreal conditions with the interest with which he hears a statement of what is actually taking place.

"In the second place, a writer who starts from arbitrarily assumed premises is in danger of forgetting from time to time their unsubstantial foundation, and of arguing as if they were true. This has been the source of much error in Ricardo. He assumed the land of every country to be of different degrees of fertility, and rent to be the value of the difference between the fertility of the best and of the worst land in cultivation. The remainder of the produce he divided into profit and wages. He assumed that wages naturally amount to neither more nor less than the amount of commodities which nature or habit has rendered necessary to maintain the laborer and his family in health and strength. He assumed that, in the progress of population and wealth, worse and worse soils are constantly resorted to, and that agricultural labor, therefore, becomes less and less proportionately productive; and he inferred that the share of the produce of land taken by the landlord and by the laborer must necessarily increase, and the share taken by the capitalist constantly diminish.

"This is a logical inference, and would consequently have been true in fact, if the assumed premises had been true. The fact is, however, that almost every one of them is false. It is not true that rent depends on the difference in fertility of the different portions of land in cultivation. It might exist if the whole territory of a country were of uniform quality. It is not true that the laborer always receives precisely the necessaries, or even what custom leads him to consider the necessaries of life. In civilized countries he almost always receives much more; in barbarous countries he from time to time obtains less. It is not true that, as wealth and population advance, agricultural labor becomes less and less proportionately productive. . . . Mr. Ricardo was certainly justified in assuming his premises, provided that he was always aware, and always kept in mind, that they were merely assumed. This, however, he seems sometimes not to know, and sometimes he forgets. Thus he states, as an actual fact, that in an improving country the difficulty of obtaining raw produce constantly increases. He states as a real fact that a tax on wages falls not on the laborer, but on the capitalist. . . .

"A third objection to reasoning on hypothesis is its liability to error, either from illogical inference or from the omission of some element necessarily incident to the supposed case. When a writer takes his premises from observation and consciousness, and infers from them what he supposes to be real facts, if he have committed any grave error, it generally leads him to some startling conclusion. He is thus warned of the probable existence of an unfounded premise or of an illogical inference, and, if he be wise, tries back until he has detected his mistake. But the strangeness of the results of an hypothesis gives no warning. We expect them to differ from what we observe, and lose, therefore, this incidental means of testing the correctness of our reasoning."[1]

With regard to the criticisms on Ricardo, I may perhaps have an opportunity of adverting to them on some future occasion. I shall merely at present say that they appear to me to be unfounded. But what I am more immediately concerned in remarking is that the objections of Mr. Senior to the hypothetical treatment of Political Economy, so far as they possess weight, do not apply to this mode of treatment as I have just described it. According to that description, Political Economy has been represented as deriving its premises from existing facts; it was to the inferences drawn from these premises only that the term "hypothetical" was applied; but as these inferences constituted the whole of what is properly called Political Economy, I conceived that Political Economy was properly designated as an hypothetical science. But it is to the character, not of the conclusions, but of the premises, that Mr. Senior's objections apply. "A writer," he says, "who starts from *arbitrarily assumed premises* is in danger of forgetting their unsubstantial foundation." "No one listens to an exposition of what might be the state of things under *given but unreal conditions* with the interest with which he hears a statement of what is actually taking place." "The strangeness of the results of an hypothesis gives no warning." It is evident that these are no objections to a system of doctrines which is founded, not on an hypothesis, but on facts.

Mr. Senior's language, indeed, would seem to imply that, if the premises have a foundation in existing facts,

---

[1] "Introductory Lecture on Political Economy," 1852, p. 63.

the conclusions logically deduced from them must represent actual phenomena. Speaking of Ricardo's reasoning, he says, " This was a logical inference, and would *consequently* have been true in fact, if the assumed premises had been true." But it is surely possible that the premises should be true, and yet incomplete — true so far as the facts which they assert go, and yet not including all the conditions which affect the actual course of events. The laws of motion and of gravity are not arbitrary assumptions, but have a real foundation in nature; and it is a strictly logical deduction from those laws that the path of a projectile is in the course of a parabola; yet, in point of fact, no projectile accurately describes this course; the friction of the air, which was not included in the premises, coming in to disturb the operation of the other principles. In the same way (as I have already shown by several illustrations, and as will appear more fully hereafter) the doctrines of Political Economy, though based upon indubitable facts of human nature and of the external world, do not necessarily represent, and scarcely ever precisely represent, existing occurrences. Indeed, Mr. Senior in another passage fully admits this. " We shall not," he says, " it is true, from the fact that by acting in a particular manner a laborer may obtain higher wages, a capitalist larger profits, or a landlord higher rent, be able to infer the further fact that they will certainly act in this manner; but we shall be able to infer that they will do so *in the absence of disturbing causes.*" This concedes the only point for which I contend — the point, namely, that the conclusions of Political Economy do not necessarily represent actual events. The facts thus being agreed upon, the question is reduced to the verbal one, viz., whether a science, the doctrines of which correspond with external realities only "in the absence of disturbing causes," is properly described as a positive or hypothetical science. It appears to me that a proposition can not correctly be said to represent "positive truth" which corresponds with facts only when no disturbing causes intervene— this condition, moreover, being one which is scarcely ever realized. Nor do I think the description would be less objectionable, even though, as Mr. Senior afterward remarks, it were "frequently" possible "to state the cases in which these causes may be expected to exist, and the force with which they are likely to operate." On the other hand, as I have already admitted, if the term be used, not with reference to what are properly the doctrines of Political Economy, but to the grounds on which these doctrines are built, Political Economy is as well entitled to be considered a "positive science" as any of those physical sciences to which this name is commonly applied.

This point, however, as I have said, is a purely verbal one, and as such is of little importance, provided the real character of the principles in question be borne in mind. This character, as I have endeavored to establish, is identical with that of the physical principles which are deduced from the laws of gravitation and motion; like these, the doctrines of Political Economy are to be understood as asserting, not what *will* take place, but what *would* or what *tends* to take place, and in this sense only are they true.[1] If this admission con-

---

[1] "Ce serait avec aussi peu de fondement et aussi peu de succès que vous attaqueriez la théorie du libre échange en alléguant que certains pays

stitute an objection to Political Economy,[1] it is equally
an objection to Astronomy, Mechanics, and to all those

---

ont atteint, sous un régime de restrictions et d'entraves, un très-haut
degré de prospérité, tandis que d'autres pays, qui jouissaient d'une liberté
de commerce comparativement fort grande, sont restés en arrière de pre-
miers dans leur développement économique.   On vous répondrait que la
prospérité économique est le résultat complexe de plusieurs causes, parmi
lesquelles il peut y en avoir de plus puissantes que la liberté.   La théorie
que vous attaquez n'est point formulée en ces termes, que *le développement
économique des sociétés est proportionnel au degré de liberté dont elles
jouissent*, mais dans ceux-ci : *que la liberté du commerce est plus favorable
à ce développement que les entraves et les restrictions*, vérité contre laquelle
votre objection ne saurait avoir aucune force, puisque les faits allégués ne
lui sont nullement contraires.   Ces faits prouvent seulement que le
développement économique est un phénomène complexe, et que, chez
les nations signalées par vous comme fournissant une preuve de l'ineffi-
cacité du libre échange, l'action de ce principe a été neutralisée par
d'autres causes, telle que la situation géographique, ou l'insécurité
résultant de mauvaises lois, qui ont agi en sens opposé."—*Précis de la
Science Économique*, Tome I. pp. 13, 14.

[1] Mr. Jennings ("Natural Elements of Political Economy," p. 4) dis-
poses of this defense of economic doctrine in the following fashion :
"The doubting pupil is now dismissed with the assurance that the principles of Political Economy which he has been taught, if not true, *have
a tendency* to be true ; that if found imperfect in the *abstract* (*quære*, concrete ?), they are perfect in the *concrete* (*quære*, abstract ?) ; and that an
allowance must always be made for the influence of disturbing causes."

I don't know that any further reply need be made to this than that
given in the text, namely, that whatever be the value of the objection, it
applies with equal force to all sciences whatever which have reached the
deductive stage.   In no other sense is a dynamical law true than as expressing "a tendency" influencing matter.   Whether the result in any
given case be such as the law asserts will depend, whatever be the branch
of speculation, upon whether the necessary *ceteris paribus*, implied in its
statement, is realized.   The reason that attention has been drawn more
to the influence of disturbing causes in the political and moral than in the
physical sciences is sufficiently obvious.   In those physical sciences which
are sciences of observation, as Astronomy, the principles are few in number and perfectly definite in character ; while in those physical sciences,
as, *e. g.*, Chemistry, in which the principles are more numerous and complex, we can avail ourselves of experiment.   In the former case all, or
nearly all, the causes influencing the result are known, and their effect
may be calculated ; in the latter, all that are not required may be elimi-

physical sciences which combine deductive with inductive reasoning.[1]

And now I am in a position to attempt a definition of Political Economy, which I would define in either of the following forms: As the science which, accepting as ultimate facts the principles of human nature and the physical laws of the external world, as well as the conditions, political and social, of the several communities of men, investigates the laws of the production and distribution of wealth which result from their combined operation; or thus: As the science which traces the phenomena of the production and distribution of wealth up to their causes, in the principles of human nature and the laws and events—physical, political, and social—of the external world.

---

nated. But in the moral and political sciences, in which we have to deal with human interests and passions, the agencies in operation at any given time in any given society are numerous, while, being in this case precluded from experiment, we are unable to prepare the conditions beforehand with a view to preserving the necessary *ceteris paribus.*

[1] See Mill's "System of Logic," book iii. chap. x. § 5.

LECTURE III.

OF THE LOGICAL METHOD OF POLITICAL ECONOMY.

§ 1. In adverting in the opening of this course to the differences of opinion now existing respecting many fundamental principles in Political Economy, I stated that these discrepancies appeared to me to be chiefly traceable to the more loose and popular method of treating economic questions which has of late years come into fashion; and I further stated that this change in the character of economic discussions was, as I conceived, mainly attributable to the practical success of economic principles in the experiment of free trade—a success which, while it attracted a new class of adherents to the cause of Political Economy, furnished its advocates also with a new description of arguments.

The method which we pursue in any inquiry must be determined by the nature and objects of that inquiry. I was thus led in my opening lectures to consider the nature and objects of Political Economy. In the present and following lectures I proceed to discuss the method which, having regard to what Political Economy proposes to accomplish, it is proper to pursue in its investigations.

Let me recall briefly the description I have given of the nature and objects of Political Economy. You will remember I defined Political Economy as the science which investigates the laws of the production and distribution of wealth, which result from the principles of human nature as they operate under the actual circumstances of the external world. I also stated that those mental principles and physical conditions are taken by the political economist as ultimate facts, as the premises of his reasonings, beyond which he is not concerned to trace the causes of the phenomena of wealth. I next considered the nature of those ultimate facts, physical and mental, and found that, although so numerous as to defy distinct specification, there are yet some, the existence and character of which are easily ascertainable, of such paramount importance in relation to the production and distribution of wealth as to afford a sound and stable basis for deducing the laws of those phenomena. The principal of these I stated to be, first, the desire for physical well-being implanted in man, and for wealth as the means of obtaining it, and, as a consequence of this in conjunction with other mental attributes, the desire to obtain wealth at the least possible sacrifice; secondly, the principles of population as derived from the physiological character of man and his mental propensities; and, thirdly, the physical qualities of the natural agents, more especially land, on which human industry is exercised. I also showed you that the most important of the subordinate principles and facts affecting the production and distribution of wealth, which come in to modify and sometimes to reverse the operation of the more cardinal principles, are also capable of being ascertained and appreciated, with sufficient accuracy at least to be taken account of in our reasonings, if not to be constituted as premises of the science; and of these also I gave several examples.

D

This, then, being the character of Political Economy, we have to consider by what means the end which it proposes—the discovery of the laws of the production and distribution of wealth—may be most effectually promoted. To the question here indicated, the answer most commonly given by those who take an interest in economic speculation is—by the inductive method of inquiry; but this, without more explanation than is usually given, affords us little practical help. For what are we to understand by the inductive method? What are the logical processes intended to be included under this form of words? That is a question to which not many of those who talk of studying Political Economy "inductively" have troubled themselves to find an answer. The truth is, the expression "inductive method" is one used with much latitude of meaning even by writers on inductive logic—latitude of meaning which it will be very necessary, before determining whether induction be applicable or inapplicable to economic investigation, to clear up. In its more restricted and, as I conceive, its proper sense, induction is thus defined by Mr. Mill: "That operation of the mind by which we infer that what we know to be true in a particular case or cases will be true in all cases which resemble the former in certain assignable respects. In other words, induction is the process by which we conclude that what is true of certain individuals of a class is true of the whole class, or that what is true at certain times will be true in similar circumstances at all times."[1] The characteristic of induction, as thus defined, is that it involves an ascent from particu-

---

[1] "System of Logic," book iii. chap. ii. § 1.

lars to generals, from individual facts to laws. But the word is frequently used, and by writers of authority, in a sense much wider than this. For example, in his History of the Inductive Sciences, Dr. Whewell invariably speaks of laws of nature, both ultimate and secondary, as being established by induction, and as being "inductions;" though from his own account of their discovery it is evident that this has frequently been accomplished quite as much by reasoning downward from general principles as by reasoning upward from particular facts. Sir John Herschel, too, not unfrequently uses the term with the same extended meaning, as embracing all the logical processes of whatever kind by which the truths of physical science are established.[1] And Mr. Mill, in speaking of the inductive logic, describes it as comprising not merely the question, "how to ascertain the laws of nature," but also, "how, after having ascertained them, to follow them to their results." Such being the large sense in which "induction" has been employed by authoritative writers, it is obvious that, as thus understood, the inductive method can not properly be contrasted with the "deductive," since it includes among its processes this latter mode of reasoning. The proper antithesis to induction, in this wider meaning of the word, would be, not deduction, but rather that method of speculation which is known as the "metaphysical," in obedience to which the inquirer, disdaining to be guided by experience, aims at reaching nature by transcending phenomena through the aid of the intuitions, real or supposed, of the human mind. If this latter mode of rea-

---

[1] "Preliminary Discourse on Natural Philosophy."

soning has ever been followed in economic speculation, it has, at least, been long laid aside by all writers of any mark (with the possible exception of Mr. Ruskin); and therefore the question really at issue, as regards the logical method proper to Political Economy, is not as to the suitability for economic investigation of the inductive method as understood by such writers as Herschel and Whewell—this we may take as generally agreed upon—but the more specific problem as to the suitability, for the purpose in hand, of the several processes included under that comprehensive sense of the phrase; in other words, to ascertain the place, order, and importance which induction (in the narrower meaning of the term), deduction, verification, observation, and experiment ought to hold in economic inquiry.

The question being reduced to this issue, the answer of not a few people would still, I apprehend, be that induction (in the narrower sense, as distinguished from deduction), in combination with observation and experiment, constitutes the true path of economic inquiry. The student, according to this view, ought to commence by collecting and classifying the phenomena of wealth, prices, wages, rents, profits, exports, imports, increase or decline of production, changes in modes of distribution: in a word, as far as they admit of determination, all the facts of wealth as presented in actual experience in different countries; and, having done so, should employ the results thus obtained as data by which to rise, by direct or indirect inference, to the causes and laws which govern them. Now, to perceive the utter futility, the necessary impotence of such a method of proceeding as a means of solving economic problems, one has only to con-

sider what the nature of those problems is. The phenomena of wealth, as they present themselves to our observation, are among the most complicated with which
speculative inquiry has to deal. They are the result of
a great variety of influences, all operating simultaneously,
reinforcing, counteracting, and in various ways modifying
each other. Consider, for example, the number of influences that go to determine so simple a phenomenon
as the selling price of a commodity—the great number
and variety of conditions comprised under the expression,
"the demand for it," the not less numerous and varied
circumstances on which the "supply" depends, any change
in any of which, if not accompanied by a compensating
change in some of the co-existing conditions, must result in a change in the actual phenomenon. Now, when
this high degree of complexity characterizes phenomena ;
when they are liable to be influenced by a multiplicity
of causes all in action at the same time; in order to establish inductively—that is to say, by arguing upward
from particular facts—the connection of such phenomena
with their causes and laws, one condition is entirely indispensable : there must be the power of experimentation
in the rigorously scientific sense of that word.[1] But this
is a resource from which the student of social and economic problems is absolutely debarred. If any one doubt
this, he has only to consider what an experiment, such
as would in physical science be accounted a sufficient
ground for a sound induction, really implies ; that it implies the possibility of finding or producing a set of
known conditions as the medium in which the experi-

---

[1] See Mill's "Logic," book iii. chap. x.

ment is performed, and which shall remain constant
during its performance. A chemist, for example, seeking to discover the character of a new substance, places
it under the receiver of an air-pump, or in a solution
carefully prepared beforehand, all the constituents of
which are accurately known to him; and submits it, thus
circumstanced, to certain influences—say to some known
changes in temperature, or to electrical or galvanic action. Having taken these precautions, he is justified in
attributing the changes which result to the causes which
have been put in operation; and the mode in which the
given substance may be affected by the agencies brought
to bear upon it is thus ascertained. Where procedure
of this kind is practicable—and it is practicable over the
greater portion of the field of physical inquiry—"the
plurality of causes" and "the intermixture of effects" do
not offer any insuperable obstacle to the interpretation
of nature by induction properly so called; it has, in fact,
been by this method that many of the most important discoveries in physical science have been made.[1] But from
any thing in the least tantamount or comparable to this,
the political economist is, I need scarcely say, necessarily
excluded. The subject-matter of his inquiries is human
beings and their interests, and with these he has no power to deal after the arbitrary fashion permissible in the
other case. He must take economic phenomena as they
are presented to him in the world without in all their
complexity and ever-changing variety; but from facts

---

[1] Discoveries, that is to say, of *ultimate* laws. As Mr. Mill has shown,
the law of complex effects is not amenable to the method of simple induction, even when experiment may be conducted under the most rigid conditions.—"Logic," book iii. chaps. x. and xi.

as thus presented, if he decline to avail himself of any other path than that of strict induction, he may reason till the crack of doom without arriving at any conclusion of the slightest value. Beyond the merest empirical generalizations, advance from such data is plainly impossible. No economic or social truth, meriting the name of scientific, ever has been discovered by such means, and it may be safely asserted none ever will be. What leads people to imagine the contrary is that in their reasoning on social and political facts they are constantly in the habit of combining with their knowledge of phenomena motives and principles of conduct so familiar that their use of them as premises in their argument escapes their notice : they employ, that is to say, quite unconsciously to themselves, their knowledge of human nature, or of physical or political conditions, as a guide in their interpretation of the facts supplied to them by the statistician, and by this means, no doubt, conclusions more or less important are sometimes arrived at; but, then, this is not to reason inductively in the strict sense of that expression, but, so far as such reasoning admits of logical analysis, to combine the two processes of induction and deduction. It so happens, however, that the deductive portion of the operation, resting as it does on familiar assumptions of which no proof is given or needed, escapes notice, while the inductive, which generally has to deal with new and perhaps striking facts, strongly arrests attention; and the opinion thus gains ground that purely inductive reasoning suffices for the establishment of truths which are really reached by a very different path.

"The vulgar notion," says Mr. Mill, "that the safe meth-

ods on political subjects are those of Baconian induction,
that the true guide is not general reasoning, but specific
experience, will one day be quoted as among the most un-
equivocal marks of a low state of the speculative faculties
in any age in which it is accredited.   Nothing can be more
ludicrous than the sort of parodies on experimental reasoning which one is accustomed to meet with, not in popular
discussion only, but in grave treatises, when the affairs of
nations are the theme.   'How,' it is asked, 'can an institution be bad, when the country has prospered under it?'
'How can such or such causes have contributed to the
prosperity of one country, when another has prospered
without them?'   Whoever makes use of an argument of
this kind, not intending to deceive, should be sent back to
learn the elements of some one of the more easy physical
sciences.   Such reasoners ignore the fact of plurality of
causes in the very case which affords the most signal example of it.   So little could be concluded, in such a case,
from any possible collation of individual instances, that
even the impossibility, in social phenomena, of making artificial experiments, a circumstance otherwise so prejudicial
to directly inductive inquiry, hardly affords, in this case,
additional reason of regret.   For even if we could try experiments upon a nation or upon the human race, with as
little scruple as M. Majendie tries them upon dogs or rab-
bits, we should never succeed in making two instances
identical in every respect except the presence or absence
of some one indefinite circumstance.   The nearest approach
to an experiment in the philosophical sense, which takes
place in politics, is the introduction of a new operative element into national affairs by some special and assignable
measure of Government, such as the enactment or repeal
of a particular law.   But where there are so many influences at work it requires some time for the influence of
any new cause upon national phenomena to become apparent; and as the causes operating in so extensive a sphere
are not only infinitely numerous, but in a state of perpetual
alteration, it is always certain that before the effect of the

new cause becomes conspicuous enough to be a subject of induction, so many of the other influencing circumstances will have changed as to vitiate the experiment."[1]

The foregoing considerations suffice to show the utter inadequacy of the inductive method, in the narrower sense of that expression, as a means of solving the class of problems with which Political Economy has to deal, arising from the impossibility of employing experiment in economic inquiries under those rigorous conditions which are indispensable to give cogency to our inductions. But if Political Economy and social studies generally are placed at this serious disadvantage as compared with the various branches of physical research, on the other hand, as I shall now proceed to show, the former studies enjoy in their turn advantages peculiar to themselves—advantages which, if duly turned to account, may perhaps be found to go some considerable way toward redressing the balance.

§ 2. Let us endeavor to realize the position of a speculator on the physical universe at the outset of physical inquiry. The most striking feature of the situation would be the extraordinary variety and complexity of the phenomena presented to his gaze, contrasted with the absence of any clear indication of the causes at work or the laws of their operation. He would find himself in the midst of a mighty maze, possibly not without a plan, but offering to the student no apparent clew by which to thread its intricacies. No wonder that in presence of such a problem the primitive thinker should have yearn-

---

[1] " System of Logic," book iii. chap. x. § 8 ; and see for a fuller discussion of the same question, book vi. chap. vii. of the same work.

ed for some comprehensive and all-explaining principle, and should have directed his efforts at once and by whatever means to supply this capital requirement. "For the human mind," says Bacon, "strangely strains after and pants for this, that it may not remain in suspense, but obtain something fixed and immovable, on which as on a firmament it may rest in its excursions and disquisitions"[1]—some ultimate force, some paramount and all-pervading principle, by intellectual deductions from which light may be let in among the confused and jarring elements of the world. Accordingly, it was to the attainment of some such "Atlas for their thoughts" that the efforts of the earliest thinkers were invariably directed. Nor were they wrong in the importance they attached to the possession of such a stand-point; only unfortunately they mistook the means of securing it, and, instead of proceeding by sap and mine, endeavored to carry the position by a *coup de main*. Each thinker made his guess. According to one, the ultimate principle was water; according to another, air; according to a third, number; and so the game went on through long ages; till at length the truth began to dawn that, as our knowledge of physical causes and laws—even of their existence—comes to us exclusively through observation of their physical effects, it is by way of those effects—through the study of physical phenomena—that the approach to the former must be made, if made at all: in other words, it began to be seen that the inductive method was the only method suitable, at all events at the outset of inquiry, to physical investigation. This truth, rec-

---

[1] "De Aug. Scien.," lib. v. cap. iv.

ognized and acted on at intervals by a few here and there, was at length proclaimed by Bacon in language which arrested the attention of the scientific world, and has become a portion of the heritage of mankind. But the point to be attended to here is that the necessity for the method of induction as the path to physical discovery arose entirely from the fact that *mankind have no direct knowledge of ultimate physical principles.* The law of gravitation and the laws of motion are among the best established and most certain of such principles; but what is the evidence on which they rest? We do not find them in our consciousness, by reflecting on what passes in our minds; nor can they be made apparent to our senses. That every particle of matter in the universe gravitates, each toward the rest, with a force which is directly according to the mass, and inversely according to the square of the distance—or that a body once set in motion will, if unimpeded by some counter force, continue forever in motion in the same direction and with unimpaired velocity—these are propositions which can only be established by an appeal to the intellect; the proof of all such laws ultimately resolving itself into this, that, assuming them to exist, they account for the phenomena. They are not the statement of any actual experiences, but, in the words of Mr. Herbert Spencer, " truths drawn from our actual experiences, but never presented to us in any of them." " Men culled," says Dr. Whewell, " the abstract rule out of the concrete experiment; although the rule was in every case mixed with other rules, and each rule could be collected from the experiment only by supposing the others

known."[1] And what is true of the laws of gravitation
and of motion is true equally of all the ultimate principles of physical knowledge. Thus the undulatory
theory of light, the theory of the molecular constitution
of matter, the doctrine of *vis inertiæ*—all alike elude
direct observation, and are only known to us through
their physical effects.

The inductive method, therefore, in the narrower sense
of the expression, formed the necessary and inevitable
path by which, having regard to the limitation of the
human faculties, physical investigation was bound, in the
outset of its career, to proceed. I say in the outset of
its career; because, so soon as any of the ultimate laws
governing physical phenomena were established, a new
path by which to approach physical problems would at
once be opened. The inquirer would have secured that
"Atlas for his thoughts" for which the earlier speculators
sighed; and the method of deduction — incomparably,
when conducted under the proper checks, the most powerful instrument of discovery ever wielded by human intelligence—would now become possible. What, accordingly, we find in the history of the most important physical sciences, is this: a long period of laborious inductive
research, during which the ground is prepared and the
seed sown, terminating at length in the discovery—most
frequently made at nearly the same time by several independent inquirers—of some one or two great physical
truths; and then a period of harvest, in which, by the
application of deductive reasoning, the fruits of the great
discovery in the form of numerous intermediate princi-

---

[1] Whewell's "History of the Inductive Sciences," vol. ii. p. 26.

ples connecting the higher principles with the facts of experience are rapidly gathered in. Thus the progress of mechanical science was slow, notwithstanding what had been done by Archimedes and the ancients, till the primary dynamical principles were established by Galileo and his contemporaries; but these once firmly seized, and the deductive process applied to the premises thus obtained, a crowd of minor discoveries in mechanics, hydrostatics, and pneumatics, all involved in the more fundamental principles, followed in rapid succession.[1] It is thus that most of those middle principles, the *axiomata media* of physical science, have been arrived at. But it is not in the discovery of *axiomata media* only that the potency of the deductive process has been exemplified. In combination with induction it has frequently been the means by which the highest physical generalizations have been reached. Of this the most eminent example is the law of gravitation itself, arrived at by Newton in the main by way of deduction from the dynamical premises supplied by the discoveries of Galileo. In effect the problem, as it came to the hands of Newton, had assumed nearly this form—to find a force which, in conjunction and in conformity with the laws of motion, will produce the planetary movements, already generalized by Kepler.[2] The law of gravitation, indeed, illustrates the potency of the deductive method in a double sense. It is at once its richest fruit and its most fruitful source. It was, as I have just intimated, a deduction from the laws of dynamics brought to the interpretation of the phenomena of the planetary movements; and, once established, it

---

[1] " History of the Inductive Sciences," book vi. chaps. iii.-vi.

[2] Ibid., book vii. chap. ii.

became the great generative principle from which, always in connection with the data furnished by observation, all the later discoveries of astronomy have been derived.

"As the discovery itself was great beyond former example, the features of the natural sequel to the discovery were also on a gigantic scale; and many vast and laborious trains of research, each of which might in itself be considered as forming a wide science, and several of which have occupied many profound and zealous inquirers from that time to our own day, come before us as parts only of the verification of Newton's theory. Almost every thing that has been done and is doing in astronomy falls inevitably under this description; and it is only when the astronomer travels to the very limits of his vast field of labor that he falls in with phenomena which do not acknowledge the jurisdiction of the Newtonian legislation."[1]

It appears, then, that the path of induction was only exclusively followed in physical research pending the discovery of ultimate laws. So soon as the first great physical generalization was established, deduction came at once into play, leading, in combination with induction and the means of verification it afforded, to a rapid extension of physical knowledge. Of course, as new physical generalizations of the higher order were established, the scope for the employment of the deductive process would be enlarged; and the effect would be a gradual change in the logical character of the physicist's problem, and by consequence in his method. At the outset of investigation the problem was—given the phenomena, to find the causes and laws, and the only feasible course

---

[1] See "History of the Inductive Sciences," vol. ii. p. 195.

of procedure was induction; but, as more and more principles were discovered, the problem came gradually to assume another form, namely this—given the phenomena
and certain causes and laws affecting them, to find the
other causes and laws implicated in the results. The
student was gradually getting possession of both ends
of the chain, and his task was being narrowed to determining the intervening links.

§ 3. I have been at pains to bring clearly before your
minds the logical nature of the physical problem as it
presented itself at the outset of speculation to the inves-
tigator of physical nature, and as it *now* presents itself,
in order that you may fairly appreciate in what degree
the analogy holds between physical investigation and
the class of inquiries with which we are here concerned.
Some pages back I remarked that if the economist was
at a disadvantage as compared with the physical investi-
gator in being excluded from experiment, he had also
some compensating circumstances on his side. The nature of these compensating circumstances will now become apparent. " *The economist starts with a knowledge
of ultimate causes.* He is already, at the outset of his
enterprise, in the position which the physicist only attains after ages of laborious research. If any one doubt
this, he has only to consider what the ultimate principles
governing economic phenomena are. As explained in
my last lecture, they consist of such facts as the following:
certain mental feelings and certain animal propensities
in human beings; the physical conditions under· which
production takes place; political institutions; the state
of industrial art: in other words, the premises of Polit-

ical Economy are the conclusions and proximate phenomena of other branches of knowledge. These are the
sources from which the phenomena of wealth take their
rise, precisely as the phenomena of the solar system take
their rise from the physical forces and dynamical laws
of the physical universe; precisely as the phenomena of
optical science are the necessary consequences of the
waves of the luciferous medium striking on the nerves
of the eye. For the discovery of such premises no elaborate process of induction is needed. In order to know,
e. g., why a farmer engages in the production of corn,
why he cultivates his land up to a certain point, and why
he does not cultivate it further, it is not necessary that
we should derive our knowledge from a series of generalizations proceeding upward from the statistics of corn
and cultivation, to the mental feelings which stimulate
the industry of the farmer, on the one hand, and, on the
other, to the physical qualities of the soil on which the
productiveness of that industry depends. It is not necessary to do this—to resort to this circuitous process—
for this reason, that we have, or may have if we choose
to turn our attention to the subject, direct knowledge of
these causes in our consciousness of what passes in our
own minds, and in the information which our senses convey, or at least are capable of conveying, to us of external facts. Every one who embarks in any industrial pursuit is conscious of the motives which actuate him in
doing so. He knows that he does so from a desire,
for whatever purpose, to possess himself of wealth; he
knows that, according to his lights, he will proceed toward his end in the shortest way open to him; that, if
not prevented by artificial restrictions, he will buy such

materials as he requires in the cheapest market, and sell the commodities which he produces in the dearest. Every one feels that in selecting an industrial pursuit, where the advantages are equal in other respects, he will select that in which he may hope to obtain the largest remuneration in proportion to the sacrifices he undergoes; or that in seeking for an investment for what he has realized, he will, where the security is equal, choose those stocks in which the rate of interest to be obtained is highest. With respect to the other causes on which the production and distribution of wealth depend—the physical properties of natural agents, and the physiological character of human beings in regard to their capacity for increase—for these also direct proof, though of a different kind, is available; proof which appeals not indeed to our consciousness, but to our senses. Thus, *e. g.*, the law of the diminishing productiveness of the soil to repeated applications of capital, if seriously questioned, is capable of being established by direct physical experiment upon the soil, of the result of which our senses may be the judges. If political economists do not perform this experiment themselves in order to establish the fact, it is only because every practical farmer performs it for them. In the case of the physical premises, therefore, of Political Economy, equally with the mental, we are entirely independent of those refined inductive processes by which the ultimate truths of physical science are established.

§ 4. The economist may thus be considered at the outset of his researches as already in possession of those ultimate principles governing the phenomena which form the subject of his study, the discovery of which in the case of physical investigation constitutes for the inquirer his most arduous task; but, on the other hand, he is excluded from the use of experiment. There is, however, an inferior substitute for this powerful instrument at his disposal, on which it may be worth while here to say a few words. I refer to the employment of hypothetical cases framed with a view to the purpose of economic inquiry. For, although precluded from actually producing the conditions suited to his purpose, there is nothing to prevent the economist from bringing such conditions before his mental vision, and from reasoning as if these only were present, while some agency comes into operation—whether it be a human feeling, a material object, or a political institution—the economic character of which he desires to examine. If, for example, his purpose be to ascertain the relation subsisting between the quantity of money in circulation in any given area of exchange transactions and its value, he might make some such supposition as this: 1, in a given state of productive industry a certain number and amount of exchange transactions to be performed; 2, a certain amount of money in circulation; 3, a certain degree of efficiency (in the sense explained by Mr. Mill[1]) in the discharge of its functions by this money; lastly, a certain addition made to the money already in circulation. These conditions being supposed, and being also supposed to remain constant, the scene of the experiment would be prepared. It is true the action of the added money can not be made apparent to the senses of the economist, or

---

[1] " Principles of Political Economy," vol. ii. p. 18.   Sixth Edition.

to those of his hearers or readers, but from his knowledge of the purposes for which money is used, and of
the motives of human beings in the production and exchange of wealth, it will be in his power to trace the
consequences which in the assumed circumstances would
ensue. These he would find to be an advance in the
prices of commodities in proportion to the augmentation
of the monetary circulation; a result from which he
would be justified in formulating the doctrine that,
other things being the same, the value of money is inversely as its quantity. Or again, supposing the object
be to ascertain the law governing agricultural rent, the
economist might take as his hypothesis the following
conditions: 1, a certain state of agricultural skill; 2, a
capacity of the soil to yield certain returns on the application of capital and labor in certain proportions; 3, a
tendency in the soil to yield diminished proportional
returns after a certain point in cultivation has been
reached; 4, different degrees of fertility in different
soils; lastly, the land owned by one class of persons,
while another, in possession of capital, desires to occupy it for the purpose of cultivation. These suppositions
being made, he would then take account of the known
motives, on the one hand, of farmers, on the other of
landlords in their dealings concerning rent, and would
deduce from these, in connection with the supposed circumstances, the amount of rent which the latter would
be content to receive and the former to pay. The conditions determining agricultural rent would thus be ascertained. It is true the conclusion arrived at would
represent hypothetical truth merely — that is to say,
would express a law true only in the absence of dis-

turbing causes; but, as I have already explained,[1] so much qualification as this must be understood of all scientific laws whatever. Putting aside mere empirical generalizations, no law of nature, it matters not whether the sphere of inquiry be physical, mental, or economic, is true otherwise than hypothetically — than in the absence of disturbing causes. The process, then, which I have been describing is one mode by which a knowledge of economic laws may be reached; and I think you will perceive that it is in the nature of an experiment conducted mentally. I am far, indeed, from saying that it is not very inferior, as an agency for the discovery of truth, to the sensible physical process for which it is the substitute; since, while the actual operations of nature can not err, there is in a hypothetical experiment always the danger, not only that some of the conditions supposed to be present may, in the course of ratiocination, be overlooked, but also of a flaw in the reasoning by which the action of the particular cause under consideration is established. And this renders it expedient that the process in question should, as far as possible, be supplemented by such sorts of verification as economical inquiry admits of. For example, it is open to the economist, having worked out his problem in the manner described, to look out for some actual instance which approximates in as many of its principal circumstances as possible to those of his hypothesis. Having found one, he can observe how far the results realized in the actual case correspond with his hypothetical conclusions; and in case, as would usually happen, the cor-

---

[1] *Ante*, pp. 69, 70.

respondence was not complete, he would have to consider how far the discrepancy admitted of being explained by reference to the presence of known disturbing causes. Unfortunately, for reasons already indicated, verification can never in economic inquiry be otherwise than very imperfectly performed; but this notwithstanding, if carefully conducted it is often capable of furnishing sufficient corroboration to the processes of deductive reasoning to justify a high degree of confidence in the conclusions thus obtained.

In this way may hypothesis be made to serve as in some sort a substitute for experiment in economic investigation; and in point of fact it has been by this means that not a few important doctrines of the science have been worked out. The writer who has employed this particular resource most freely and with the most effect is Ricardo; nor could a more decisive proof be given of the ignorance generally prevailing on the subject of method in Political Economy than is furnished by the flippant attacks which have been made upon this eminent thinker from so many quarters on this account. In employing the method of reasoning on hypothetical cases, Ricardo, in effect, employed, as far as the nature of his problem and the circumstances of the case permitted, that experimental method which those who would disparage his great achievements affect to extol, but the real nature of which, as their criticisms show, they so little understand. Here is an example of the manner in which he could wield this instrument of economic research. The question under consideration was the fundamental principle of international trade, and Ricardo wished to show that it might be the interest of a country to import an article from another, even though it were in its power to produce the imported article itself at less cost than it was produced at in the country from which it came. This, at first view, paradoxical position, Ricardo thus by means of a simple hypothesis (which, while it divested the problem of all its accidental complications, brought into clear light the few essential conditions on which its solution depended) was enabled to establish; it being evident that, under the supposed circumstances, the known motives of men in the pursuit of wealth could only lead to the very result asserted. "Two men," he says, "can both make shoes and hats, and one is superior to the other in both employments; but in making hats he can only exceed his competitor by one fifth, or 20 per cent., while in making shoes he can excel him by one third, or 33 per cent.; will it not be to the interest of both that the superior man should employ himself exclusively in making shoes, and the inferior man in making hats?"[1]

In further confirmation of what I have said as to the nature of the ultimate premises of the physical sciences in contrast with those of Political Economy, I would ask you now to consider the different use to which hypothesis is put in the former department of knowledge. In Political Economy, as we have just seen, hypothesis is used in order to supply the reasoner mentally with those known and constant conditions which are essential to the development deductively of the fundamental assumptions of the science, but from the production of which in actual existence he is precluded by the nature of the

---

[1] Ricardo's Works, McCulloch's edition, p. 77.

case ; and in this way, as I have explained, it may be regarded as a substitute for experiment ; in physical investigation, on the other hand, as the required conditions can actually be produced, there is no need to assume them hypothetically, and accordingly this is never done. For what purpose, then, is hypothesis used in physical research ? Always as a means of arriving at ultimate causes and laws. Such causes and laws not being susceptible of direct proof, through an appeal to the consciousness or senses, conjecture, guess, hypothesis, is the natural, as it is in truth the only possible path by which they may be reached. Accordingly, the physicist frames an hypothesis as to the nature of those causes and laws, and having done so, proceeds to bring together conditions fitted to test the correctness of his guesses—that is to say, he institutes experiments to verify his hypothesis. Such a course would be obviously unsuitable in the analogous case in economic investigation. No one thinks of framing an hypothesis as to the motives which induce men to engage in industry, to prefer remunerative to unremunerative occupations, or to embark their earnings in investments which, *ceteris paribus,* promise the best returns ; or, again, as to the causes which, in a given state of agricultural knowledge and skill, set a permanent limit to the application of capital and labor to the soil ; any more than as to those on which depend the continuance and growth of population. Conjecture here would manifestly be out of place, inasmuch as we possess in our consciousness and in the testimony of our senses, as I have already shown, direct and easy proof of that which we desire to know. In Political Economy, accordingly, hypothesis is never used as a help toward the discovery of ultimate causes and laws; just as in physical investigation it is never used as a substitute for experiment.[1]

Such, then, are the positions respectively of the economist and of the physical philosopher with reference to the logical nature of the problem with which each has to deal. And this being so, what can argue greater ignorance of the conditions of the case—at once of the real nature of the precedents furnished by the physical sciences, and of the character of the economic problem, than to appeal to the former, as is constantly done, in justification of the exclusive use of the purely inductive method in economical research. It is to overlook alike the peculiar weakness and the peculiar strength of the economist's position. It is to advocate for Political Economy a method which is only powerful in physical investigation, because the physicist can employ it in connection with conditions from the realization of which the economist is from the nature of his inquiry precluded; and to refuse to employ an engine of discovery ready to our hands, which the physicist has spent centuries of laborious speculation in his efforts to attain, and which, once possessed, has proved the most potent of all his appliances. What the precedents of physical science, rightly understood, teach the economist is to regard deduction as his principal resource; the facts furnished by observation and experience being employed, so far as circumstances permit, as the means of verifying the conclusions thus obtained, as well as, where discrepancies are found to occur between facts and his theoretical reasonings,

---

[1] See Appendix C.

for ascertaining the nature of the disturbing causes to which such discrepancies are due. It is in this way, and in this way only, that the appeal to experience is made in those physical sciences which have reached the deductive stage—that is to say, which in the logical character of their problems present any real analogy to economic science.

§ 5. In connection with the processes just referred to of verification and the discovery of disturbing causes, or (to express the same idea differently) the discovery of the minor influences affecting economic phenomena, we find the proper place of statistics in economic reasoning. Statistics are collections of facts arranged and classified with a view to particular inquiries; and it is by availing ourselves of this systematized method of observation that we can most effectually check and verify the accuracy of our reasoning from the fundamental assumptions of the science; while the same expedient offers also by much the most efficacious means of bringing into view the action of those minor or disturbing agencies which modify, sometimes so extensively, the actual course of events. The mode in which these latter influences affect the phenomena of wealth is, in general, unobvious, and often intricate, so that their existence does not readily discover itself to a reasoner engaged in the development of the more capital economic doctrines. In order to their detection, therefore, attention must be drawn to the effects which they produce; and this, as I have said, can be best done by the use of statistics in constant connection with deductive ratiocination.

It is important to observe that the relation of statistics

E

to Political Economy is in no respect different from that
in which they stand to other sciences which have reached the deductive stage.   The registered observations of
the astronomer are the statistics of astronomy, which it
is his business to compare with the conclusions theoretic-
ally evolved from the dynamical principles constituting
the premises of his science, and for purposes strictly analogous to those which have just been described.[1]   In
those sciences, indeed, which admit of experiment, as,
e. g., chemistry, formal statistics are little used.   Statistics
here are unnecessary, because experiment affords, only in
a more efficacious way, the means of instituting the same
comparison.   But what are known by the chemist as
"residual phenomena" are precisely analogous to those
discrepancies between the conclusions of the economist
and the facts of the statistician to which I have been
adverting, and lead in the same way to the discovery of
new elements or principles before overlooked.

Such is the method of investigation which the nature
of the evidence available in economic inquiry, as well as

---

[1] " For example : the return of the comet predicted by Professor Encke,
a great many times in succession, and the general good agreement of its
calculated with its observed place during any one of its periods of visibil-
ity, would lead us to say that its gravitation toward the sun and planets
is the sole and sufficient cause of all the phenomena of its orbitual motion ;
but when the effect of this cause is strictly calculated and subducted from
the observed motion, there is found to remain behind a *residual phenomenon,* which would never have been otherwise ascertained to exist, which is
a small anticipation of the time of its reappearances or a small diminution
of its periodic time, which can not be accounted for by gravity, and whose
cause is therefore to be inquired into.   Such an anticipation would be
caused by the resistance of a medium disseminated through the celestial
regions ; and as there are other good reasons for believing this to be a
vera causa, it has therefore been ascribed to such a resistance."—*Herschel's
Natural Philosophy,* p. 156.

the analogy of the physical sciences, so far as they correspond with it in the logical character of their problems, suggest as proper to be followed in Political Economy; and such also is the method which has in fact been followed, whether it has been distinctly stated or not, by all those writers, from Turgot and Adam Smith to Mr. Mill, who have contributed most effectually to the advancement of economic knowledge. The detailed evidence for this statement, however, may be fitly reserved for another lecture.

LECTURE IV.

OF THE LOGICAL METHOD OF POLITICAL ECON-
OMY.—(*Continued.*)

§ 1. I CONCLUDED my last lecture by remarking that
the method of investigation which—guided by the nature of the evidence available in economic inquiry, as
well as by the analogy of physical sciences, so far as this
is pertinent—we found proper for Political Economy, is
also the method which has in fact been followed, whether
formally avowed or not, by those writers who have contributed most effectually to the progress of economic
knowledge. The course taken by these thinkers may, in
general, be thus described. Those principles of the science which require no proof, depending directly upon
consciousness, as, for example, the desire to obtain wealth
at the least sacrifice, they have, in general, silently assumed, proceeding at once to argue on them without
formally stating them. Those which are liable to dis-
pute, such as the physical properties of productive agents,
and the physiological character of human beings in relation to their capacity of increase, they have established
by such evidence as is suitable. The celebrated essay
of Malthus on Population, *e. g.*, is almost wholly devoted
to the establishment and illustration of the two latter
principles—viz., the capacity of human beings to multiply their species, and the capacity of the earth under as-

sumed conditions of agricultural skill to yield subsistence. The foundations of the primary principles being thus laid, they have proceeded to consider the consequences which result in the production and distribution of wealth; how these principles, coming into action under the guidance of human intelligence, lead naturally to the division of labor, to the mutual interchange of products among the different producers, to the use of money as a medium of exchange, and, as communities advance, to the rise of rent, and the slower progress of population. They have proceeded then to trace the general laws of value, of rent, of profits, and of wages, which result from the operation of the same principles. But the conclusions thus arrived at being frequently found to differ in various degrees from the observed facts, their attention has thus been drawn (in strict conformity with the order which I have described) to the influence of subordinate principles in modifying the force of the more powerful causes. Thus, the chapter of Adam Smith on the different rates of wages in different employments is wholly an inquiry into the nature and force of such secondary principles. The chapter of Ricardo on " Foreign trade," and those of Mr. Mill on " International values," are inquiries of a similar character; the object being to discover those special causes which, in the case of international exchanges, intervene to modify the general laws of value. Again, Mr. Senior's essay " On the Cost of obtaining Money" is an example of the same kind.

But perhaps the best example which has yet been furnished of the proper use of statistics in the advancement of economic science is afforded by Mr. Tooke in his well-

known "History of Prices." One of the first and most
elementary principles in the theory of money is that, *ceteris paribus,* the value of money is inversely as its quantity. In the discussions which took place during the
earlier part of the present century on the phenomena of
prices and the circulation, this principle was assumed as
true, not simply hypothetically—*i. e.,* in the absence of
disturbing causes—but as representing the sole, or at least
principal, cause regulating general prices. By the ultra-
bullionists on the one hand, and by the advocates of an
inconvertible currency on the other, it was alike taken
for granted that all fluctuations in the prices of commodities are to be attributed, at least in a principal degree,
to alterations in the amount of money, including under
that term coin and bank-notes.[1] Now the result of Mr.
Tooke's elaborate examination of the commercial and
monetary history of that period was to show that no
such correspondence between prices and the circulation
as these different authorities assumed was, in fact, to be
found. Here, then, was an example of that discrepancy
between the conclusions of abstract reasoning and actual
phenomena which it is the business of statistical investi-

---

[1] To such an extent did this delusion prevail, that the celebrated Bullion
Committee of 1810, in its admirable though not faultless report, finding
that the note circulation had at that time increased in amount, and concluding from other considerations that it was excessive, took it for granted, without inquiry, that "the prices of all commodities had risen." (Report, p. 11.) I say without inquiry, 1st, because no witnesses with reference to this point were examined; and, 2d, because, had they inquired, it
is certain they would have found the facts to be precisely the reverse of
what they had assumed; the reaction consequent upon the excessive speculation of 1809 and 1810 having then taken place, and the general markets
being in a state of extraordinary depression. *Vide* Tooke's "History of
Prices," vol. i. chap. v. section 2. Mr. Huskisson, in his "Question, etc.,
Stated," also makes the same assumption.

gation to bring to light. The inevitable inference, therefore, was, either that the logical process by which these
conclusions had been established was unsound, or that
some cause influencing the phenomena had been overlooked.[1] Mr. Tooke showed that a mistake in both these
respects had been committed: 1st, a mistake of reasoning which failed to discriminate between the character
of money (properly so called)[2] in its effect upon prices,
and that of convertible notes issued by banks in the dis-
count of bills; and, 2d, a mistake in overlooking the disturbing influence which other forms of credit, equally
with bank-notes, when employed as purchasing power,
exercise upon prices. The further investigation of this
question by Mr. Tooke has resulted in a theory of prices
which, as regards the connection between prices and the
note circulation, directly reverses some of the former
maxims—asserting, for example, that the amount of the
note circulation, instead of being the efficient cause
which determines the general level of prices, is itself an
effect of this phenomenon, the fluctuations in which do
not follow but precede the fluctuations in the circula-

---

[1] It is not to be supposed that the discrepancy alluded to goes the length
of invalidating the elementary law that, *ceteris paribus,* the value of money
is inversely as its quantity. This still rests upon the same basis of mental
and physical facts as every other doctrine of Political Economy, and must
always constitute a fundamental principle in the theory of money. It
merely showed that in the practical case the condition *ceteris paribus* was
not fulfilled. The fact in question is no more inconsistent with the economic law, than the non-correspondence of a complex mechanical phenomenon with what a knowledge of the elementary laws of mechanics might
lead a tyro to expect is inconsistent with these elementary laws. A
guinea dropped through the air from a height falls to the ground more
quickly than a feather; yet no one would on this account deny the doctrine that the accelerating power of gravity is the same for all bodies.

[2] See Tooke's "History of Prices," vol. iv. chap. ii. section 2.

tion; and, in addition, affording for the first time an explanation of a large and important class of monetary phenomena.

Such, then, is the method of inquiry in Political Economy, which not only the nature of the case suggests, but which analogy and authority alike support.

§ 2. In order to illustrate more clearly the character of this method, and the assistance which a clear apprehension of it may afford in discussing economic questions, I shall now take a particular example of an economic law, and examine the nature of the assertion which it contains, and the kind of proof by which it may be established or refuted.

It is a very fundamental law in Political Economy that "cost of production regulates the value of freely produced commodities." By the "cost of production" of a commodity, I may as well explain, is meant the labor, abstinence, and risk which is necessary in order to produce that commodity; and by the expression "freely produced commodities" is to be understood commodities which may be produced in any required quantity by any one who chooses to go to the trouble and expense of producing them. This, then, being the meaning of the words, let us consider what is the nature of the assertion which is made when it is said that "cost of production regulates value."

Is it meant that freely produced commodities invariably and without exception exchange for one another in proportion to their respective costs of production?— in other words, that in every instance in which such commodities are exchanged their costs of production are precisely equal? If this is what the doctrine means, the assertion is clearly untrue. Wheat and barley, *e. g.*, in England are freely produced commodities, and a stone of average wheat will, at present prices [1856–57], exchange for little more than a stone of average barley; but the cost of producing a stone of wheat is very much greater than the cost of producing a stone of barley; so much so that a farmer does not consider himself to be equally well paid if he does not obtain nearly half as much more for the former. Again, take another interpretation: does the doctrine mean that, taking the average of considerable periods, the value of freely produced commodities will be constantly proportioned to the costs of producing them? Neither in this sense can the doctrine bear strict examination. Cotton goods, *e. g.*, in England, and tobacco in America, are freely produced commodities. Any one who has the requisite means at his disposal may engage in the production of either to any extent he pleases; yet in the exchange of tobacco and manufactured cotton between America and England, even taking the average of long periods, the proportions in which they exchange will not be found to correspond with their respective costs: the quantity of English manufactured cotton which will exchange for a given quantity of American tobacco will, on an average, represent a greater cost.

In what sense, then, is the statement true that cost of production regulates the value of freely produced commodities? The answer is, it is true hypothetically—in the absence of disturbing causes; or, to express the same thing in a different form, the doctrine expresses not a matter of fact, but a tendency. Thus, to revert to my former example, it is not true, as a matter of fact, that wheat and barley at present exchange in proportion to their respective costs of production; for the quantity of wheat for which a given quantity of barley will exchange represents the result of a greater expenditure of labor and abstinence; but it *is* true that wheat and barley *tend* to exchange in proportion to their costs of production;[1] and the proof of this is that the present high price of barley, as compared with that of wheat, will lead to an increased growth of barley and a diminished growth of wheat next season. It may be that the change in the comparative quantities produced will not be sufficient to bring their values into proportion with their costs, in which case a still further increase will take place in the growth of barley the following year, and a still further diminution in the growth of wheat; or it may be that the change will exceed what is necessary, and that the value of barley as measured in wheat may fall below what its cost of production would require; and in this case the process in the succeeding year will be reversed. But, whatever be the result, and however calculation may be defeated by the vicissitudes of the seasons and by other causes, the tendency of its value to approach the cost of its production will be constant and unfailing.[2] It is, to borrow Mr. Mill's illustra-

---

[1] When the cost of producing agricultural produce is spoken of as determining its value, the reader will understand that I always speak of the cost of that portion *which is raised at greatest expense.*

[2] It is contended by Mr. Macleod ("Theory and Practice of Banking," vol. i. p. 13) that it is not the cost of production which regulates the value of agricultural produce, but the value which regulates the cost. It is, no doubt, true that in the case of agricultural produce a rise in its value, or (supposing the value of money to be constant) in its price, is generally fol-

tion, like the tendency of the ocean to a level, which is
as constant and certain as the law of gravitation, though

---

lowed by an increased cost of production. On the other hand, a rise in
the price of a manufactured article generally leads to a diminished cost;
and it would be just as reasonable to say that price regulates cost of production in one case as in the other. What price really regulates is the
quantity that shall be produced; an advance in the price of an article beyond its normal level always indicating that the supply is insufficient, and
thus leading to increased production. Now it so happens that, in the case
of agricultural produce, the smaller the quantity required the less the proportional cost at which it can be obtained, it being the less necessary to
resort to any but the most fertile soils; and hence it arises that every advance in price, leading to increased production, is followed generally by
increased cost. On the other hand, in the case of manufactured articles,
the larger the scale of production, the less generally the proportional cost,
owing to the greater room thus afforded for the use of machinery and the
division of labor; and, accordingly, the advance in price in this case, leading also to extended production, is generally followed by a diminished
cost.

It is evident that in neither case is the cost regulated by the price, but
by the quantity required, together with the physical and mechanical conditions under which the article is produced. On the other hand, it is certain that, in both cases, cost is the regulator of price, since whatever be
the cost at which the quantity required is produced—whether it be raised
or lowered by the extended production—this cost is the point about which
the price will permanently oscillate.

Mr. Macleod says that the doctrine that cost of production regulates
value means "that a perseverance in producing any article at great expense, if continued long enough, would in the end succeed in raising its
value." Mr. Macleod, of course, means "continued long enough" at an
unremunerating price (for if the price were remunerating, it would be in
proportion to cost of production, and there would be no point in the argument); but such a case is economically impossible. All Ricardo's reasonings—indeed, the reasonings of all economists that I have met with except Mr. Macleod—proceed upon the assumption that self-interest is the
motive to production. A case, therefore, which supposes "a perseverance in producing" without an adequate remuneration—that is to say,
without an adequate motive — is simply out of the pale of Political
Economy. Cost of production would not indeed, under the circumstances
supposed, regulate value; but no more would demand and supply, nor any
other principle that can be imagined. "Value," in short, would no longer
have any meaning, since exchange, with the feelings of self interest which
dictate it, would cease to exist.

probably no single square yard of its surface may even
for a moment actually attain it. In the example, however, which I have given of the relative value of barley
and wheat within the United Kingdom, though the proportions in which these two articles exchange may never
at any given moment strictly conform to their costs of
production, still, if the average were struck over an extensive period, the correspondence would probably be
found to be in most cases sufficiently accurate; just as
the average elevation of a cork thrown on the surface of
the ocean would be found to represent the level which
the whole surface constantly tended to approach. But
in the other example of the exchange of cotton goods
and tobacco between England and America, this would
not be the case. As I have already observed, if we
were to take the average proportions in which these two
articles are exchanged even over a considerable period,
this average would not be found to correspond with
their respective costs of production.

Is it, then, true that the law fails in this instance? I
answer that it no more fails than the law of gravitation
fails when its force is neutralized by the action of friction. The law operates, but its operation is controlled
by the force of another principle which intervenes and
modifies the resulting phenomena. The case affords an
example of a statement which I made on a former occasion, that a law in Political Economy, though logically
deduced from indubitable facts of nature, is yet, when
applied to external phenomena, true only hypothetically. Thus the law that cost of production regulates the
value of freely produced commodities is a doctrine logically deduced from the unquestionable facts that men

desire physical well-being, and are averse to unrequited toil. Looking simply to these principles, it clearly follows that men desire to obtain wealth at the least possible outlay of labor; and consequently that they will not continue to give an article, the production of which costs a given amount of labor, for an article which may be obtained on less onerous terms; and this is only in other words to say that cost of production regulates value. But this is only true on the hypothesis that no other principle intervenes to disturb the direct operation of the two principles just described. For example, love of country may intervene to disturb their operation. An Englishman may prefer permanently to exchange a pound of manufactured cotton for a quantity of raw tobacco which costs less labor, rather than to go to America to grow tobacco for himself. In international dealings, therefore, a new principle, love of country, comes into play, and modifies the action of the primary principles from which the law of cost has been deduced; the result is a deviation of international values from the course which the elementary law would lead us to expect. To recur to the illustration just employed—let us suppose a weight to remain in equilibrium on an inclined plane. No one who understood the meaning of a physical law would say that there was here any failure of the law of gravitation: the law does not fail, but is counteracted by the intervention of another force, friction. And similarly there is no failure of the law of cost of production, when in international trade friction of another kind intervenes to modify the results of its operation. Diminish the friction of the plane in the physical example, and the weight will begin to descend in obedience to the law of gravitation. And, in precisely the same way, diminish the obstructions to international communication, diminish the force of international prejudices, and the general laws of value will be found immediately to act, and international values will approach more nearly to the respective costs of production of the articles exchanged.

From this conception of an economic law, as expressing a hypothetical, not a positive, truth ; as representing, not what actually takes place, but what *tends* to, or *would* take place in the absence of disturbing causes, we can have no difficulty in perceiving the *kind* of proof on which such a law rests, and the *kind* of arguments, therefore, by which alone, if questioned, it can be refuted.

Not being an assertion respecting the order of economic phenomena, it can neither be established nor refuted by an appeal to the records of such phenomena—that is to say, by statistical or documentary evidence bearing on the course of industrial or commercial affairs ; but, expressing a tendency deduced from certain principles of human nature as they operate under certain physical conditions, it can be established only by proving the existence of such principles and conditions, and showing that the tendency asserted follows as a necessary consequence from these data ; or, if questioned, can be refuted only by showing, either that the principles and conditions assumed do not exist, or that the tendency which the law affirms does not follow as a necessary consequence from this assumption. In economic reasonings, therefore, supposing the logical portion of the process to be sound, the appeal must in all cases ultimately be to consciousness or to some external fact —to some mental or physical law. And this, in fact, has been the kind of proof by which all those principles of Political Economy that can be considered as received doctrines have been established, and the issue to which, in the works of its ablest cultivators, all controverted questions have been ultimately reduced.

§ 3. The readers of the "Wealth of Nations" will remember the passage near the opening of the work, in which the existence of the division of labor is traced to certain principles in human nature coming into operation under the actual circumstances in which mankind are placed. Having referred to the means of persuasion employed by the lower animals in order to gain the favor of those whose services they require, Adam Smith continues:

"Man sometimes uses the same arts with his brethren; and, when he has no other means of engaging them to act according to his inclinations, endeavors, by every servile and fawning attention, to obtain their good will. He has not time, however, to do this upon every occasion. In civilized society, he stands at all times in need of the co-operation and assistance of great multitudes, while his whole life is scarce sufficient to gain the friendship of a few persons. In almost every other race of animals, each individual, when it is grown up to maturity, is entirely independent, and in its natural state has occasion for the assistance of no other living creature; but man has almost constant occasion for the help of his brethren, and it is in vain for him to expect it from their benevolence only. He will be more likely to prevail if he can interest their self-love in his favor, and show them that it is for their own advantage to do for him what he requires of them. Whoever offers to another a bargain of any kind proposes to do this. Give me that which I want and you shall have this which you want, is the meaning of every such offer; and it is in this manner that we obtain from one another the far greater part of those good offices which we stand in need of." [1]

Similarly, it was by appealing to the principle of self-interest as it operates in commercial transactions, and to the physical properties of the precious metals as portable commodities, that the same writer overthrew the dogmas of the mercantile system, and established the doctrines of free trade:

"No commodities," he tells us, "regulate themselves more easily or more exactly according to the effectual demand than gold and silver; because, on account of the small bulk and great value of those metals, no commodities can be more easily transported from one place to another — from the places where they are cheap to those where they are dear."

... "A country," he continues, "that has no mines of its own must undoubtedly draw its gold and silver from foreign countries, in the same manner as one that has no vineyards of its own must draw its wines. A country that has wherewithal to buy wine will always get the wine it has occasion for; and a country that has wherewithal to buy gold and silver will never be in want of those metals. They are to be bought for a certain price like other commodities, and as they are the price of all other commodities, so all other commodities are the price of those metals. We trust with perfect security that the freedom of trade, without any attention of government, will always supply us with the wine which we have occasion for; and we may trust with equal security that

---

[1] "Wealth of Nations," McCulloch's ed., 1850, p. 7.

it will always supply us with all the gold and silver which we can afford to purchase or to employ, either in circulating our commodities or in other uses :[1]

the reason, though not expressed, being clearly implied that the same self-interest which is sufficient to induce the wine producers in France and Spain to send us their wines, will be sufficient also to induce the producers of gold and silver to send us these metals, if, as in the former case, we are prepared to give them their value in return.

Again, reasoning against another doctrine of the same school — that the regulation of trade by a system of duties and prohibitions was indispensable to the commercial prosperity of the country—Adam Smith thus argues :

"This is to direct private people in what manner they ought to employ their capitals, and must in almost all cases be either a useless or a hurtful regulation. If the produce of domestic can be bought there as cheap as that of foreign industry, the regulation is evidently useless. If it can not, it must generally be hurtful. It is the maxim of every prudent master of a family never to attempt to make at home what it will cost him more to make than to buy. The tailor does not attempt to make his own shoes, but buys them of the shoemaker. The shoemaker does not attempt to make his own clothes, but employs a tailor. The farmer attempts to make neither the one nor the other, but employs those different artificers. . . . What is prudence in the conduct of a private family can scarce be folly in that of a great kingdom. If a foreign country can supply us with a commodity cheaper than we ourselves can make it, better buy it of them with some

---

[1] "Wealth of Nations," McCulloch's ed., 1850, p. 190.

part of the produce of our own industry employed in a way in which we have some advantage. The general industry of the country being always in proportion to the capital which employs it, will not thereby be diminished, no more than that of the above-mentioned artificers, but only left to find out the way in which it can be employed with the greatest advantage. It is certainly not employed to the greatest advantage when it is directed toward an object which it can buy cheaper than it can make. The value of its annual produce is certainly more or less diminished when it is thus turned away from producing commodities evidently of more value than the commodity which it is directed to produce." [1]

In all this reasoning, I need scarcely remark, the appeal throughout is to the principle of self-interest. Restrictions on trade, if not useless, are hurtful—are prejudicial to the increase of national wealth, because in the operations of trade men naturally seek their own interest, and, consequently, if left to themselves will naturally employ their industry in that way in which they have some advantage; the general industry of a country, therefore, will not be diminished by freedom of trade, but only be employed to most advantage—which is to say, in other words, employed so as to produce the greatest possible amount of wealth.

It is true, Adam Smith afterward refers to historical facts, and adduces the cases of Spain and Portugal to show the prejudicial effect of the mercantile system on the trade of those countries. You will observe, however, that when he has recourse to history, it is always in illustration or confirmation; he never makes it the

---

[1] "Wealth of Nations," p. 200.

basis of his doctrines. He first lays the foundation deep in the principles of human nature and the physical facts of the external world; the subsequent reference to historical events is merely in illustration of the mode in which the laws thus established operate.

Take another example from one of our greatest economic discoverers. One of the most important discoveries in Political Economy which has been made since the time of Adam Smith is the theory of foreign trade established by Ricardo. "Previous to this," as Mr. Mill observes, "the theory of foreign trade was an unintelligible chaos." The discovery of Ricardo was briefly this—he showed that the circumstance which determined an interchange of commodities between two nations was not, as had previously been supposed, a difference in the *absolute* cost of producing the commodities exchanged, but a difference in the *comparative* cost. Corn and iron, *e. g.*, might both be obtained at less cost in Sweden than in England, and yet no exchange of corn and iron would necessarily take place between Sweden and England; but if the comparative costs of iron and corn were different in those two countries, the principles of self-interest would inevitably lead to an exchange. I have already quoted the passage[1] in which Ricardo, illustrating this position by a simple hypothesis, was enabled to establish it as a doctrine of economic science by a direct appeal to the motives which engage men in the production and exchange of wealth.

So also, in discussing with M. Say the theory of rent,

---

[1] *Ante*, p. 94.

of profits, of taxation, the question is invariably reduced
by Ricardo, either to some acknowledged principle of
human action, or to some question of physical fact—
to such issues, *e. g.*, as the following : What is the productive capacity of the soil ? Is the ratio of returns to
outlay, *ceteris paribus*, the same, or greater, or less, as
the outlay is increased ? Does not the conduct of farmers in resorting to inferior soils prove it to be less ?
In the cultivation of land, therefore, is there not a point
at which the returns pay the capital and labor employed in cultivation, and no more ? Will not the self-interest of farmers lead them to push cultivation to this
point ? Will not the same consideration prevent them
from pushing it further ? Are there not soils of every
possible degree of fertility ? Are there not some, therefore, which will merely yield an average profit on the
outlay, and no more? Will not the competition of farmers, each guided by considerations of individual self-interest, force up the rent of land till the returns merely
leave them the average rate of profits on their capital ?
Will not the same motive prevent them from raising it
further ? Is not rent, therefore, determined by the difference between the cost of that portion of agricultural
produce which is raised at greatest expense and that
which is raised at less? Supposing a tax on raw produce—the farmer will not pay the tax, for then he
would not get the average profits, and rather than sub-
mit to less his self-interest will lead him to withdraw
his capital from the land. Will he evade the tax by
contracting the area of cultivation and giving a lower
rent ; or will the wants of consumers induce them to
give a higher price rather than diminish their consump-

tion ?   Will, therefore, the minimum rate of profit, necessary in order to secure the investment of the farmer's capital, be maintained by a fall in rent, or by a rise in price ?   On the decision of such points are the laws of rent, of profits, of taxation, made to turn.

These examples, which might be multiplied at pleasure, will suffice to show the *kind* of proof on which the great masters of Political Economy have rested their discoveries, and the *kind* of issues to which they have reduced their controversies.   In every case, where the logical process of an opponent is admitted as correct, the appeal has ultimately been to some mental or physical principle : their method has thus been strictly in conformity with what the nature of an economic law, as I have described it, would require.

LECTURE V.

§ 1. IN treating in my last lecture of the method of inquiry proper to Political Economy, I was led to an examination of the nature of the assertion contained in an economic law, and of the kind of proof needed for establishing or refuting it. On these points I arrived at the following conclusions, viz., that an economic law expresses, not the order in which phenomena occur, but a tendency which they obey; that, therefore, when applied to external events, it is true only in the absence of disturbing causes, and consequently represents a hypothetical, not a positive truth; that, being deduced by necessary consequence from certain mental and physical principles, it can be established only by establishing the existence of the principles assumed, and showing that by logical necessity they involve the tendency asserted; and refuted only by proving that the principles do not exist, or that the reasoning is unsound. In all these respects I endeavored to show that the character of an economic law is strictly analogous to that of those laws of physical nature which are obtained, or which may be obtained, by deduction from the ultimate principles of the sciences to which they belong.

So far, then, the analogy between a "law" as understood in Political Economy and a "law" as understood in the more advanced physical sciences holds good. In the present lecture I propose to call your attention to a circumstance in which this analogy fails, and to the consequences which result from this failure in the development of economic truth. In both departments of speculation alike a law of nature expresses a tendency constantly influencing phenomena; but in the physical sciences the discovery of a law of nature is never considered complete till, in addition to the general tendency, an exact numerical expression is found for the degree of force with which the tendency in question operates.

"It is the character," says Sir John Herschel,[1] "of all the higher laws of nature to assume the form of precise quantitative statement. Thus the law of gravitation, the most universal truth at which human reason has yet arrived, expresses not merely the general fact of the mutual attraction of all matter; not merely the vague statement that the influence decreases as the distance increases, but the exact numerical rate at which that decrease takes place; so that, when its amount is known at any one distance, it may be calculated exactly for any other. Thus, too, the laws of crystallography, which limit the forms assumed by natural substances, when left to their own inherent powers of aggregation, to precise geometrical figures with fixed angles and proportions, have the same essential character of strict mathematical expression, without which no exact particular conclusions could ever be drawn from them."

To give one example more, the use of the balance has brought chemistry into the category of those sciences the laws of which admit of quantitative statement.

---

[1] "Natural Philosophy," p. 123.

The chemist is consequently able, not merely to describe the general nature of the reaction which will take place between certain substances under known conditions, but can give beforehand a numerical statement of the exact proportions in which the several elements will unite in the resulting compound.

This is a degree of perfection, however, which it does not seem possible that Political Economy, any more than jurisprudence, philology, or any of those branches of speculation which derive their premises from the principles of human nature, should ever attain.[1] For, although the general character of these principles may be ascertained, and although when stated with sufficient precision they may be made the basis of important deductions, yet they do not, from the nature of the case, admit of being weighed and measured like the elements and forces of the material world : they are therefore not susceptible of arithmetical or mathematical expression ; and hence it happens that, in speculating on results which depend on the positive or relative strength of such principles, perfect precision, numerical accuracy, is not attainable.   Political Economy seems on this account necessarily excluded from the domain of exact science.[2]

---

[1] This remark might, perhaps, be extended to embrace the organic sciences in general.   The laws of organic development, for example, expressing general tendencies, are never formulated in other than general terms. See "Habit and Intelligence," by J. J. Murphy, vol. i. pp. 201, 202, 212.

[2] Mr. Macleod considers Monetary Science (which he appears to regard as commensurate or nearly so with Political Economy) as "an exact science."   In the Introduction to his "Theory and Practice of Banking," vol. ii. p. 25, he writes as follows : "These principles then act with unerring certainty—they are universally true—human instinct is as certain, invariable, and universal in its nature as the laws of motion—AND THAT IS THE CIRCUMSTANCE WHICH RAISES MONETARY SCIENCE TO THE RANK OF

This quality of economic doctrines will be made more clear by a few examples.

AN EXACT OR INDUCTIVE SCIENCE. It is this which renders it possible to establish it upon as sure, solid, and imperishable a basis as mechanical science. Alone of all the political sciences its phenomena may be expressed with the unerring certainty of the other laws of nature." (The capitals are the author's.) Mr. Macleod seems to confound an "exact" with a positive science. In order that a science be "exact," it is necessary, not only that its premises be "universal and invariable," but, further, that they be susceptible of precise quantitative statement. If Mr. Macleod can show that *both* these conditions are satisfied in the present instance—that the character of "human instinct" can be known, and also that its force can be measured, as the force of gravitation—he will then have established a basis for an exact science of Political Economy.

Mr. Jennings, in his " Natural Elements of Political Economy," appears to take the same view. "Our instruments," he says, "though acting on and through the principles of human nature, are found to consist of metallic indices [money] related as parts and multiples, and not less capable of being made subservient to the processes of exact calculation than are the instruments of any purely physical act. The results of these principles when observed may be expressed in figures; as may also the anticipated results of their future operation, or such relations as those of Quantity and Value, Value and Rate of Production, may be exhibited in the formulæ and analyzed by the different methods of Algebra and of Fluxions" (pp. 259-260).

There is no doubt that economic results, *when they have happened*, may be expressed in figures; but I apprehend something more than this is requisite to render a science "exact." Mr. Jennings indeed adds, "as may also the *anticipated* results of their future operation;" but the question is, Have we such data as will warrant us in accepting as trustworthy the results thus obtained? Will our calculations turn out, not merely generally, but "exactly" true? Instead of dealing in general terms, let us take a specific case—the determination of the price of corn—and consider what in this instance would be necessary in order to arrive at an "exact" result. The following is taken from Tooke's "History of Prices:" "But, further, supposing that both the results of the harvest and the stock on hand were made known with sufficient approach to accuracy by government returns, there would yet remain the greatest uncertainty in the corn markets unless the probable extent of the supplies from abroad could be known. And, granting all these grounds for estimates of actual and forthcoming supplies to be within the power of government to ascertain, there would be yet another influence on prices—and consequently a cause of fluctuation—namely, the speculative views operating on the minds of both buyers and

F

The decline of profits, as nations advance in wealth and numbers, is a circumstance which has long attracted the attention of economists. It has also been observed that, in the course of this progress, a minimum point is attained, beyond which profits do not further decline;

---

sellers in the contemplation of circumstances likely to affect the produce of the next ensuing harvest. From the time of sowing to that of gathering the wheat crop, the casualties of the weather exercise an influence on the markets, and thus cause fluctuations at critical periods of the season. Among the claims put forth for agricultural statistics, it has been required, as a part of the information insisted upon, that there should be periodical government returns of the appearance of the growing crops.

" These, and other contingencies more or less important, are causes of fluctuation from uncertainty of supply. But assuming, for mere argument sake, the statistics of supply to be perfect, there still remain the uncertainties of demand.

"For the reasons which I have before stated, the variations of *consumption* are on a much smaller scale than those of supply ; but the *demand* on the markets may occasionally have a considerable temporary influence on prices, as in the case of the autumn of 1854, of the millers and bakers trying to get into stock, after having left themselves bare. There may likewise be a demand for Exportation to France or to other parts of the Continent. How could any information from government have supplied the statistics of such a demand ? But adopting the extreme and extravagant hypothesis that all these elements of uncertainty admitted of having great light thrown upon them by statistics and other information published by government, there would still remain to be solved the problem of what the price ought in consequence to be ; and this, I will venture to say, will be found to be an insoluble problem."—Vol. v. pp. 88, 89.

In order that the problems of Political Economy should be made subservient to " exact" treatment, it would be necessary, not only that " the instruments, on and through which the principles of human nature [in the pursuit of wealth] act," should be capable of quantitative measurement, but also that the principles themselves, as well as the conditions under which they come into operation, should be susceptible of exact numerical statement. The most perfect system of weights and measures would never have made chemistry an exact science, if the law of equivalent proportions had not been discovered.

Some forcible remarks in the same sense will be found in the "Philosophie Positive," tome iv. pp. 512, 513. The attempt to employ mathematical formulæ in inquiries of the social order M. Comte regards as " l'involontaire témoignage dé.isif d'une profonde impuissance philosophique."

and, further, that this minimum is different in different nations. In China, it is stated that profits show no tendency to fall below 30 per cent. per annum; while in England profits have fallen perhaps to 10 per cent., in Holland probably lower, and in other countries the decline has been arrested at other points. Now the point in the descent at which the fall is arrested—that is to say, the minimum rate of profit which can for any considerable time exist in any community—is determined by the strength of a principle which Mr. Mill has called "the effective desire of accumulation." This "effective desire of accumulation" is a general expression to denote the degree in which a desire for wealth predominates over those principles of human nature which obstruct its operation—such as the love of ease, and the desire for immediate enjoyment. When a man employs his wealth as capital for the purpose of producing more wealth, he is induced to do this—to abstain from the present enjoyment of what he has accumulated, and to engage in the toils and anxieties of business—by the prospect of adding to the sum-total of his wealth the profit which is to be made by the productive employment of it. If he had not this prospect of profit, he would not employ his acquired wealth for productive purposes at all. He would have no motive to do so. He would either consume it as he had need for it; or, if he wished to reserve some for consumption in future years, instead of adventuring it without prospect of profit in productive operations, he would convert it into money, and lay it by in some secure place, from which he could withdraw it as occasion required. Now, since the prospect of profit is that which induces a man to overcome

his natural indolence and to repress his desire for immediate enjoyment, it is evident that the minimum rate of
profit which shall suffice for this purpose will depend on
the relation in which the accumulative propensity in his
nature stands to the principles which oppose it—that is
to say, to his love of ease and inclination toward immediate enjoyment.   The stronger relatively be the former
principle, the smaller will be the prospect of gain adequate to induce him to engage in the production of
wealth—in other words, the lower may profits fall before the decline will be arrested through the absence of
sufficient motive.   The case, then, stands thus : Owing to
certain conditions incident to the character of productive agents, there is a tendency in profits to decline as
nations advance in wealth and population ; there is also
a point at which the fall is arrested, which point is determined by the strength of the effective desire of accumulation.   All the knowledge we are capable of attain-
ing on the subject resolves itself into the general fact—
that such tendencies exist, and that such results depend
on such conditions ; but, as we have no means of ascertaining the precise strength, positive or relative, of the
principles on which the result depends—independently
of the manner in which their operation is exhibited in
particular cases—we are unable to say beforehand at
what point they may be brought into equilibrium : that
is to say, we are unable to say before trial what may be
the minimum of profits which is possible in any given
community.   Contrast this with the precision attainable
in physical science.   When an astronomer speculates on
the course of a comet through space, he does not content
himself with stating the broad fact that the meteor is

under the influence of certain antagonistic forces—that it tends to fly off from the sun under the influence of the momentum with which it is carried, but that at a point in its career the force of gravity will overcome this momentum, and that at this point its course will be reversed; the astronomer not only tells us this, but tells us, further, the precise distance which the comet must travel before the force of gravity overcomes the momentum with which it moves so as to arrest its outward course; and he is able to do so, because he not only knows, as a general fact, that those tendencies represented by the laws of gravitation and motion exist, but also is able to obtain an exact numerical expression for the force with which each operates—a degree of precision which is not attainable in the determination of the principles of Political Economy.

Take another example of the uncertainty which, owing to this indefiniteness in the premises, attaches itself to the character of the conclusions of economic science.

We know, as a general rule, that human beings will more readily dispense with the luxuries and vanities than with the necessaries of life; and we may infer with certainty that, in the absence of disturbing causes, a diminution in the supply of the ordinary food of a country will be followed by a greater proportional rise in its price than a corresponding diminution in the supply of an article of less imperative necessity—that a diminution, *e. g.*, of one third in the supply of wheat will cause a greater rise in the price of wheat than a proportional diminution in the supply of silk will produce on its price. Some writers, indeed, have attempted to go beyond this general statement, and have expressed in a tabulated form the rise in the price of food which takes place in the event of certain assumed deficiencies in its quantity. Thus, according to the calculation of Gregory King, who lived in the latter end of the seventeenth century, a deficiency of one tenth in the ordinary supply of the staple food will cause a rise in its price to the extent of three tenths above the ordinary rate; a deficiency of two tenths a rise of eight tenths; a deficiency of three tenths a rise of 1.6; and so on up to a deficiency of one half, which, it is calculated, will produce a rise in price equal to four-and-a-half times the ordinary rate.[1] If, however, we consider for a moment the causes on which a rise of price depends, and the circumstances which determine its extent, it will be evident that no reliance can be placed on the accuracy of such calculations; the conditions essential to such accuracy not being susceptible of realization.

The rise which occurs in the price of wheat in consequence of a deficiency in quantity will depend (the amount of the deficiency being given) on two conditions

---

[1] The following is Gregory King's table:

Defect.		Above the common rate.
1 tenth		3 tenths.
2 tenths		8 tenths.
3 tenths	raises the price	1.6.
4 tenths		2.8.
5 tenths		4.5.

On this Mr. Tooke remarks: "It is perhaps superfluous to add that no such strict rule can be deduced; at the same time there is ground for supposing that the estimation is not very wide of the truth, from observation of the repeated occurrence of the fact that the price of corn in England has risen from 100 to 200 per cent. and upward, when the utmost computed deficiency of the crops has not been more than between one sixth and one third below an average, and when that deficiency has been relieved by foreign supplies."—"History of Prices," vol. i. p. 13.

—1st, the disposition of the people among whom the deficiency takes place to sacrifice other gratifications which it may be in their power to command to the desire of obtaining the usual quantity of their accustomed nutriment; and, 2d, the extent of the means at their disposal for obtaining other kinds of gratification—that is to say, their general purchasing power. Now if we could obtain an exact measure of this disposition, as well as of the means of giving effect to it at the command of consumers, and knew also the exact extent of the deficiency in the supply of wheat, we might then give a precise numerical statement of the rise of price which would take place under the assumed circumstances. But it is evident that none of these conditions can be accurately fulfilled. Without dwelling upon the difficulty of ascertaining accurately the other data essential to the solution, namely, the extent of the purchasing power of a community, and the mode of its distribution among different classes, it is evident that the disposition of people to sacrifice one kind of gratification to another—to sacrifice vanity to comfort, or decency to hunger—is not susceptible of precise measurement, and can never, like the forces of physical nature, be brought within the limits of a formulated statement.

This character of indefiniteness which belongs to the premises of Political Economy is very strikingly exhibited in the effect which an alteration in the duty on taxed articles sometimes produces on their consumption. It is often found, *e. g.*, that a reduction in the duty on an article of consumption—say tobacco—is followed by an increase in the total proceeds of the tax, but that if the reduction be continued further, the returns will decline. Now if the disposition and purchasing power of the community with regard to tobacco, as compared with other articles of general consumption, were known, and could be accurately expressed by a mathematical formula, the precise point at which the proceeds of a tax upon tobacco would attain their maximum could be determined beforehand; and an immense reform, without risk of failure, could at once be effected in our fiscal system. But as we have no means of ascertaining with precision the disposition of mankind, or any portion of them, in this respect, we are obliged to have recourse to a series of tentative experiments, and must content ourselves with a rough approximation to the required maximum, obtained perhaps at the cost of considerable loss to the revenue and of inconvenience to the public.

I have thought it well to call attention to this source of imperfection in our economic reasonings, as it appears to me desirable that we should know the weakness as well as the strength of our position as political economists, that we may not, by affecting an accuracy that is unattainable, bring suspicion and discredit on the undoubted truths of the science.

The celebrated formula of Malthus, as you are aware, asserted that population tends to increase in a geometrical, subsistence in an arithmetical ratio. In advancing this statement, Malthus really intended nothing more, as every candid and intelligent reader of his work will at once perceive, than to give definiteness to our conceptions of an important principle; the conclusions which he based upon the principle thus expressed not in the least depending for their truth on the mathematical accuracy of the formula. His opponents, however, were not in the humor for making this allowance. The doctrine had been stated in mathematical form, and it must, therefore, be maintained in all its strictness, or the speculations of Malthus must be forthwith pronounced a delusion, and his conclusions the phantasms of a diseased imagination.

§ 2. Such, then, being the character of an economic law, analogous in all respects to those laws of physical nature which are obtained by a similar process of deductive reasoning, with the important exception that it does not admit of quantitative statement, we are now in a position to understand how far economic laws can be made available in the explanation of economic phenomena.

The explanation of a phenomenon, or the solution of a problem (the expressions being equivalent), consists in a reference of the fact to be solved or explained to some known or acknowledged principles. The velocity of a planet through space, *e. g.*, is said to be explained when this velocity is shown to be the result of known dynamical principles. The physical phenomenon of dew is said to be explained when it is shown that the known laws of the radiation and conduction of heat, together with the laws of the condensation of watery vapor, necessarily under certain external conditions lead to the occurrence of dew; these conditions being the same as those under which, in fact, dew is observed to appear. If we admit the existence of the laws, we see that the phenomenon must be present when, in fact, it is present. In the same way the economic phenomenon of rent is said to be explained when it is shown to be the necessary consequence of the play of human interests trafficking in an article having the peculiar physical properties which are found to reside in land. In this case, also, if we admit that human beings in their dealings with land act with a view to their own interests, and, further, that the best soils in point of fertility and situation are not unlimited in supply, and that the yield to be obtained from a limited area is also not unlimited, but diminishes in proportion to the outlay, as the quantity raised is increased, we see—or by reasoning on these facts we may see—that the phenomenon of rent must present itself in the progress of society, and that it will rise and fall from those causes which we find in fact to affect it. So far, the solution of an economic problem is strictly analogous to that of a physical problem; in each case the process consists in tracing back the fact to be explained to its source in the ultimate principles of the science; if it be a physical fact, to the ultimate laws of physical nature; if an economic fact, to the ultimate axioms of Political Economy—that is to say, to the mental and physical principles from which its doctrines are derived. Until this connection is clearly established, no physical or economic phenomenon can be said to be explained.

The solution of a problem may be regarded as perfect when the principles to which it is referred are shown to exist, and to lead by necessary consequence to the precise fact which constitutes the problem to be solved.[1]

---

[1] " In such a case," says Sir John Herschel, " when we reason upward till we reach an ultimate fact, we regard a phenomenon as fully explained; as we consider the branch of a tree to terminate when traced to its insertion in the trunk, or a twig to its junction in the branch; or, rather, as a

Supposing our reasoning to be correct, it is evident that imperfection may yet arise either from the indefiniteness of our knowledge of the laws which operate in producing the phenomenon, or from ignorance of the precise circumstances under which they come into operation. With the exception, perhaps, of astronomy, there is no science that has attained absolute perfection in both these respects. Most of the advanced physical sciences, however, satisfy the first condition, though they generally fail of complete accuracy in the latter. To revert to a former example—the formation of dew—the laws of the radiation and conduction of heat and of the condensation of watery vapor on which that phenomenon depends may be accurately ascertained and expressed in mathematical formulæ ; but the circumstances under which the phenomenon appears—the state of the atmosphere, and the condition of the various bodies on which the deposition of dew takes place during any given night—can not be accurately ascertained. Now, while this is so, the solution of the problem is not complete ; since, although we may perceive from our knowledge of the laws of heat and of aqueous vapor that dew under the actual circumstances must appear, yet, from want of precision in our knowledge as to what the actual circumstances are, we can not tell the precise quantity that ought, in obedience to these laws, to be deposited ; and, therefore, can not be certain that our solution may not

---

rivulet retains its importance and its name till lost in some larger tributary, or in the main river which delivers it to the ocean. This, however, always supposes that, on a reconsideration of the case, we see clearly how the admission of such a fact, with all its attendant laws, will perfectly account for *every particular.*"—" Natural Philosophy," p. 163.

be more or less than adequate; nor whether there may not be other causes affecting the result which we have omitted to notice.

In Political Economy we have seen that the laws which it announces do not admit of precise quantitative statement: we have now further to note that the remaining portion of the data necessary to the solution of a given problem, namely, the circumstances under which they come into operation, though generally susceptible of measurement could they be ascertained, yet in practice can seldom be ascertained so completely as to admit of being stated numerically.

Take, *e. g.*, an economic phenomenon which has excited much speculation lately among economists and commercial men — the export of silver from Europe to the East, which has been proceeding on an extraordinary scale during the last year (1856). Many causes may be assigned, which, taken together, will go a certain way in accounting for this fact. There has been, in the first place, a general rise of wages in the United Kingdom — the consequence partly of our general commercial prosperity, partly of the gold discoveries — leading to an increased money demand here for the productions of Eastern countries. There has been, in the next place, a failure in the silk crop on the Continent, obliging Europeans to obtain a large portion of their silk from India and China, and thus increasing the liabilities of Europe in those quarters. The interruption of our trade during the Russian war, again, has obliged us to resort to the same quarters for linseed and other articles which we usually procure from Russian sources; leading to a further augmentation of our liabilities in the East. There is then a Chinese rebellion, tending to increase the passion for hoarding so prevalent in Oriental countries. In addition to all these causes, there are the new supplies of gold from California and Australia, lowering its value in relation to silver, displacing thereby the latter metal from the circulation of countries which have a double standard (such countries being principally confined to the continent of Europe), and thus, by lessening the demand for, lowering the value of, silver. Having regard to these different circumstances, and to the play of human interests in the pursuit of wealth to which they give occasion, it may be easily shown that the export of silver from Europe to the East (unless counteracted by some other causes of equal efficacy in an opposite direction) must take place as a necessary consequence; and, taking them altogether, and the scale of their magnitude as far as it can be ascertained, they probably go far to explain the existing drain. But are they adequate to a complete explanation? or are they more than adequate? and is it, therefore, necessary to look out for some cause acting in an opposite direction, in order to a complete explanation of the result which we witness?

Or, take another example — the high price of corn during the last four years (1853 to 1856 inclusive). Among the causes which have been assigned in explanation of this phenomenon is the fall which has recently taken place in the value of gold, the effect of the large influx from Australia and California. Some writers, however, who are of opinion that gold has not fallen in value, maintain that the high range of price is sufficiently accounted for by the shortness of supplies consequent upon the great deficiency of the harvest of 1853 over the whole of Europe, in conjunction with our exclusion from some of the usual sources of supply during the Russian war; and this notwithstanding the influence of free trade operating powerfully in the opposite direction. Now, if Political Economy were an exact science, this question could be at once determined by calculating the effect of the causes assigned, and comparing the result of the calculation with the actual market price. But, for the reasons I have explained, such a calculation transcends its resources; for even though it were possible to obtain accurate and trustworthy statistics of the production and importation of corn during the period in question, we should yet be unable to say what effect this would produce on price, from the essential indefiniteness of the other premises involved in the problem —the relative strength of human desires, the extent of the means at the disposal of consumers, not to mention the various circumstances influencing opinion as to the prospects of the coming crop, such as the changes in the weather and the reports of the harvests from other countries.[1] We are, consequently, in arguing this question, obliged to have recourse to arguments of a probable, and often of a conjectural nature, the conclusions from which must, of course, partake of the same merely probable and conjectural character, and can, therefore, never attain to that precise and definite form which distinguishes the conclusions of physical science.

§ 3. I have dwelt thus at some length on the character of an economic problem, and the degree of per-

---

[1] See Tooke's " History of Prices," vol. v. part i. sec. 29, in which the question is very fully and very satisfactorily discussed.

fection of which its solution is susceptible, because it appears to me that, among those who in the public press and elsewhere engage in economic discussions, there are few who seem to have any clear conception of what it is which, in the investigation of the phenomena of wealth, Political Economy proposes to accomplish. The following very just observations, taken from a paper in the *Statistical Journal* of October last by my immediate predecessor, Mr. Walsh, on the export of silver to the East, will illustrate the confusion of ideas to which I have adverted: "There is a mode in which some persons deceive themselves into the belief that they are accounting for this phenomenon, which calls for our consideration. I have seen it put forward by persons signing themselves 'China Merchants,' 'Eastern Merchants,' and the like — names which seem to claim authority for the bearers in a question relating to a trade with which they are conversant. They state *what* is occurring, and then imagine they have told us *why;* while, in fact, all their labor ends in telling us silver is exported to the East, because silver is exported to the East. One announces (in a letter to the *Economist,* February 2, 1856) that the direct answer to the question as to the cause of the export of silver is that the metal presents just now the most lucrative branch of commerce; and he rejects any speculations that aim at offering further explanation. The answer is quite correct, but as trifling as true. If the trade were not lucrative, no one would continue to carry it on; but the question is, what makes it unusually lucrative? and on that subject the writer does not inform us. Others wander into long descriptions of the machinery by

which the transmission of silver is effected—bills drawn
on this place for debts due elsewhere; and goods sent
to one locality in return for what is transmitted to some
other; and finally flatter themselves they have told us
why, when they have merely mentioned *how*. Why is
such a one crossing the ferry? Because he is carried in
the boat. But why did he get into the boat? That is
the question to be answered. And so, in like manner, it
is no answer to the question why silver is exported to
the East, to state the channels and appliances by which
it is transmitted. What is really required to be known
is not the machinery of transfer, but what set that machinery in motion:" in other words, what those physical facts or events are, which, in conjunction with the
self-interest of men operating in the pursuit of wealth,
produce the actual result—the drain of silver.

Every one, I suppose, has met with antagonists who,
when hard pressed with an economic difficulty, have
taken refuge in the convenient maxim that "in the end
things will find their level"—an explanation which
does not leave upon the mind a very definite notion of
the means by which the desiderated level is to be attained. A writer in the *Examiner*[1] turns to almost
equal account the words "stimulate" and "absorb,"
making them available in the support of some very extraordinary doctrines. Among other paradoxes, this
writer maintains that not only has gold not fallen in
value in consequence of the recent discoveries, but that
it has never fallen in consequence of former discoveries; and not only this, but that there is nothing in the

---

[1] December 13, 1856.

cheapened cost of producing gold which tends to lower its value. Having assumed (in disregard of such statistics as he gives) that the increased production of gold has hitherto had no effect upon prices, the writer thus proceeds to account for the fact : "The additional supply of the precious metals has stimulated the industry of the world, and in fact produced an amount of wealth, in representing which they have been themselves, as it were, absorbed." Further on he says : "But the produce of Australian and Californian gold, as well as that of silver which has accompanied it, [1]

---

[1] As if in compensation for the prevalent disposition to rest economic principles on statistical data, the writer in the *Examiner* reverses the process, and endeavors to deduce from economic principles (or what he takes for them) matters of fact which are capable of being proved by statistical evidence. In this way, in the article from which I have quoted, he attempts to prove that the stock of silver in the world has, since the Australian and Californian discoveries, been increased by an amount equal to £118,750,000. The following is his argument :

The increase of gold he takes during the last nine years as £125,000,000 ; but silver in relation to gold has during that interval risen only 5 per cent. ; therefore the stock of silver has increased by the same amount (viz., £125,000,000) *minus* 5 per cent., or £118,750,000 ; adding, in further explanation, that the rise in the price of silver would "act as a premium on its production."

It is evident that the suppressed premise of this argument is, that the relative quantities of the two metals vary always directly as their values ; but on this assumption the increase in the stock of silver would be very much greater than the *Examiner* makes it out : since, according to all estimates on the subject, the stock of silver in existence in 1848, when the Californian discoveries took place, was at least one half greater than that of gold. If, then, the correspondence in their values indicates a like correspondence in their relative quantities, instead of an addition of £118,750,000 to the stock of silver previously existing, we should have an addition of £178,125,000, or an average annual production of silver since 1848 of about £22,000,000.

But, in the next place, the assumption of a constant connection between the quantity and the value of the precious metals is directly at variance with the doctrine which it is the object of the article to establish—name-is likely to go on, and it may be asked if this must not in course of time produce depreciation. We think it certainly is not likely to do so. . . . On the contrary, it will surely be *absorbed* by increasing wealth and population as fast as it is produced."

It is strange that the obvious *reductio ad absurdum* should not have restrained such speculations. The theory applies to every conceivable augmentation of gold.

---

ly, that an increased production of gold has no tendency to affect its value. The writer starts by assuming that the value of silver must be regulated by its quantity, and then proceeds to prove that the quantity of gold can have no influence on its value. Gold, we are told, has not fallen in value, notwithstanding the increase in its quantity, and then it is argued that silver must have increased in quantity *pari passu* with gold, or else its value would not have fallen with the value of gold.

Had the writer taken the trouble to refer to the statistics which are available on the subject, he would perhaps have seen reason to doubt the soundness of his economic views. If the reader will turn to the sixth volume of Tooke's "History of Prices," Appendix XXVI., he will find returns of the importation of silver from the various producing countries during the last eight years, and estimates from these and other sources of the total annual production during the same time, in a compendious and convenient form. From these it appears that the annual production of silver, which, according to M. Chevalier's estimate, was £8,720,000 in 1848, will, in the opinion of Mr. Newmarch, based upon the statistics which he has given, have risen to about £12,000,000 for the present year—being equivalent to an increase of about 37 per cent. on the previous annual supply ; the annual supply of gold during the same period having increased by about 300 per cent.

There seems indeed every reason to suppose, from the facts stated by M. de Humboldt and M. Chevalier, in their treatises on the Production of the Precious Metals, respecting the silver mines in Mexico and Peru still unworked, as well as from the recent discoveries of quicksilver in California, cheapening as it will so considerably the cost of producing silver, that the production of silver will be rapidly extended, and that thus the depreciation now going forward in the value of gold will be concealed by the contemporaneous depreciation in the value of that metal with which it is most usual to compare it. As to the rise in the price of silver " acting as a premium on its production," this is merely the common fallacy of confounding price and value.

The stimulus is represented as in proportion to the increase of supply. Consequently, however great the increase, in the same degree will be the stimulus—in the same degree, therefore, the amount of wealth produced, and, as in representing this the gold is absorbed, in the same degree the absorption. According to this theory, then, if gold were produced in such quantities as to be as abundant as copper—nay, if it were as common as the sand on the sea-shore, it would nevertheless be as valuable as ever, and a given quantity of gold would still command the same quantity of all other things.

It is to be regretted that the writer did not favor us with his notion of the manner in which the alleged "stimulus" to industry operates, and the supposed "absorption" is effected. The stimulus, it seems, is not felt, according to the popular view, in a rise of price; for this, he asserts, the new gold has no tendency to produce: nor does it take place through an increase of demand, for this could only manifest itself through a rise of price; nor does it operate through a fall in the rate of interest, for it is notorious that during recent years the rate of interest has been high; while, with regard to the *modus operandi* of "absorption," we are equally left in ignorance.[1]

---

[1] As another example of the kind of "solutions" with which writers on economic questions satisfy themselves, take the following from the *Economist*, June 20th, 1857, p. 682. The writer is explaining the principles which regulate the distribution of the precious metals: "From the beginning of society, and in all countries, gold and silver have been used as money. They are, in fact, by some writers called natural money. If this be a true description of them, they must be distributed by natural laws, and one nation can not have more of them than another, any more than one man can have more atmospherical air than another. Europe, generally, is in a state of civilization which makes gold the most conven-

Such attempts at an explanation of economic phenomena remind us of some of the physical speculations

---

ient metal for its coin ; Asia, generally, is in a state of civilization which
makes silver the most convenient metal for its coin. Europe can not possibly have all the gold and all the silver too. Gluttonous as it may be—
led astray as its inhabitants still may be by the old theories of wealth—
the desire to keep for itself all the gold and silver that Providence sends
for all the nations of the earth can not possibly be gratified ; and so we
see the large new supplies of the precious metals pretty fairly distributed
over all. Gold comes from America and Australia into Europe ; and
silver, displaced by it, goes from Europe to Asia, to India and China,
spreading natural money every where. So, by the bounty of Providence,
the useful instruments of life in society are distributed by two streams
running in different directions over all the earth. Man is the agent for
making the distribution, but he is not conscious of all the effects he produces."

Observe the reasoning in this passage : Gold and silver have in all
countries been used as money ; they have been *called natural* money ;
therefore (assuming the designation as correct, which the writer does) they
must be distributed by natural laws ; and *therefore* one nation can not
have more of them than another. Now, in the first place, whether gold
and silver be distributed according to "natural laws," can not in the least
depend upon whether they have been properly called " natural money."
Paper credit, *e. g.*, has never been called " natural money," nevertheless
it is governed by natural laws as certainly as gold and silver ; if it were
not so, the attempt to regulate the paper currency would be an absurdity.
It is only in so far as things are governed by natural laws known to us—
that is to say, it is only in so far as we know that certain effects will follow from certain causes—that we can hope to control them.

But, secondly, it is argued that, because gold and silver are distributed
by natural laws, therefore "one nation can not have more of them than
another, any more than one man can have more atmospherical air than
another." In the first place, it is not easy to see what the connection is
between "natural laws" and equal distribution of the commodities which
are subject to these laws ; but, secondly, it is not true that one nation has
no more of the precious metals than another ; indeed, it is so palpably untrue, that it is scarcely possible to believe that the writer could have meant
what he so distinctly asserts. What, then, does he mean by saying that
one nation can not have more of the precious metals than another? Does
he mean that the share of each is in proportion to its population? or in
proportion to its trade? In neither of these senses is the doctrine more
true than in the former. The trade of England is far greater than that
of France, but the quantity of the precious metals in France is greater

of the schoolmen. Dr. Whewell mentions a doctrine maintained by these philosophers that a vessel full of ashes would contain as much water as an empty vessel.

---

than in England; and the quantity in India, in proportion to its trade, is immeasurably greater than in either England or France. Neither is the relation of the precious metals to population more constant than in their relation to trade. Will it be said that what is intended is that the precious metals are distributed among the different nations of the world *in proportion to their requirements for them?* This is true; but to give this as an explanation of the principle according to which the distribution takes place is to show that the writer does not understand in what consists the solution of an economic problem. To adopt his own illustration, it is just as if a person, when asked according to what principle the air is distributed around the globe, should reply, according to the degree of pressure operating upon it. What we want to know is, in the one case, *what* the conditions are which produce the pressure on which the dispersion of the atmosphere depends; and, in the other, *what* those requirements are which determine the distribution of the precious metals—we want to know, in short, *what* principles of human nature they are which, operating upon *what* external facts, produce the result which we see.

So far with regard to the precious metals generally; next, with regard to the metals severally, we are told that silver goes to Asia, while gold remains in Europe, because " Europe is in a state of civilization which makes gold the most convenient metal for its coin, while Asia is in a state of civilization which makes silver the most convenient metal for its coin." Now it is certain that no important change has taken place in the relative civilization of Europe and Asia, and I may add, of America, during the last ten years. If the principle, then, were a good one, silver would have been displaced in Europe long ago; and inasmuch as "the civilization" of America has been equally in advance of Oriental nations, silver would never have been the chief currency there. But silver has been the principal currency in both France and America until recently, and might be so still in spite of their "civilization," were their mint regulations framed with a view to retaining it.

Had the writer of this passage a clear conception of what it is which Political Economy proposes to accomplish, the tracing of the phenomena of wealth up to definite human motives and ascertained external facts, he would scarcely have satisfied himself with such an explanation as I have quoted—an explanation which, in the vagueness of its phraseology and the looseness of its reasoning, is much more allied to the puerile conceits and verbal quibbles of the schoolmen, than to the rigor and precision of thought which modern science demands.

The mysterious capacity of "absorption," which in this case was attributed to the ashes, is by the political economist of the *Examiner* attributed to wealth and population.

Whether in Political Economy or in physical science, before proceeding to account for a phenomenon, it is well to ascertain the fact of its existence. This preliminary point being settled, the problem is to be solved, not by vague phrases and wholesale assumptions, but by connecting the phenomenon to be accounted for with the ultimate principles of the science to which it belongs; and, in the case of Political Economy, these are certain known propensities of human nature and certain ascertained facts of the external world.

LECTURE VI.

OF THE PLACE AND PURPOSE OF DEFINITION IN POLITICAL ECONOMY.

§ 1. The present will be a convenient occasion on which to offer some remarks on the place and purpose of Definition in Political Economy. In it, as in all scientific undertakings comprising in their purview facts and objects of much variety, an arrangement of such facts and objects in classes according to the relations and affinities which, estimated with reference to the ends of the particular inquiry, happen to be most important, forms an indispensable help in the task of investigation; and, the phenomena having been classed, the separate groups need to be marked by distinct names. In these two operations consists the process of defining in positive science. Of the two, it need scarcely be said, the former, classification, is incomparably the more important, as it is also very much the more difficult operation. As has just been intimated, the problem it involves is to arrange the phenomena comprised in the particular investigation according to the relations and affinities most important with reference to the purpose in hand. A difficulty, however, meets us here at the threshold. For, in order to do this, a knowledge of such relations and affinities, and of their comparative importance in the inquiry, is plainly indispensable. But this is just what a student of nature—it matters not what may be the department of inquiry—can not possibly at the outset of his enterprise possess. What, then, is to be done? Simply what the circumstances of the case prescribe—adopt some rough provisional arrangement such as, regard being had to the end and purpose of the inquiry, the superficial appearances of things suggest; and then, as in the course of investigation new relations are brought to light and more important distinctions disclose themselves, employ the larger knowledge thus obtained to correct and amend the original draught. These being the necessary conditions under which every new inquiry must be conducted, it follows that classification, except by the merest accident, can not in the early stages of a positive science be otherwise than extremely imperfect; and, secondly, that the students of such a science must be prepared for the necessity of constantly modifying their classifications and, by consequence, their definitions with the advance of their knowledge, in order to bring them into correspondence with the larger views and more exact ideas which this advance involves; nor can they ever be sure that their arrangements are definitive, so long at least as their science stops short of absolute perfection.

§ 2. "Nomenclature, in a systematic point of view," says Sir John Herschel (pp. 138, 139), "is as much, perhaps more, a consequence than a cause of extended knowledge. Any one may give an arbitrary name to a thing, merely to be able to talk of it; but to give a name which shall at once refer it to a place in a system, we must know its properties; and we must have a system large enough and regular enough to receive it in a place which belongs to it, and to no other. It appears, therefore, doubtful whether it is desirable, for the essential purposes of science, that extreme refinement in systematic nomenclature should be insisted on. Were science perfect, indeed, systems of classification might be agreed on, which should assign to every object in nature a place in some class, to which it more remarkably and pre-eminently belonged than to any other, and under which it might acquire a name, never afterward subject to change. But, so long as this is not the case, and new relations are daily discovered, we must be very cautious how we insist strongly on the establishment and extension of classes which have in them any thing artificial as a basis of a rigid nomenclature; and especially how we mistake the means for the end, and sacrifice convenience and distinctness to a rage for arrangement."

Now all this is quite as applicable to Political Economy as to any physical science. The first inquirers into the laws of the production and distribution of wealth could not know at the outset of their inquiries what arrangement of the facts and objects forming the subject-matter of their problem would best conduce toward its solution. They could only therefore adopt that arrangement which was at the moment most promising, and this, previous to the scientific investigation of the phenomena, would naturally be the very classifications which popular discussions on political and social affairs had rendered familiar. But as investigation proceeded, and the more fundamental relations of things under their economical aspect were brought to light, the necessity for new arrangements of the phenomena, and a corresponding modification of economic language, would become apparent; and thus economic terms would come to be employed in senses sometimes narrower, sometimes more extended, than the popular use. It is manifest from this that great elaboration of definitions, at all

G

events in the early stages of investigation, is a mistake.
It is not only for the most part labor thrown away, as
subsequent inquiry will in all probability furnish reasons for largely modifying the earlier classifications,
however carefully drawn up; but, as Sir John Herschel
intimates has happened in physical science, it may even
act as a positive hinderance to the progress of knowledge
by giving an artificial rigidity to nomenclature at a time
when it is most important that it should be flexible and
elastic. It will accordingly be found that the writers
who have done most for Political Economy in its early stages have troubled themselves but little with definitions. The number of definitions, for example, to
be found in the economical writings of Turgot, Adam
Smith, and Ricardo, might be counted on the fingers.
This, however, is no argument against the gradual introduction of a scientific nomenclature into this science as
the progress of our knowledge reveals the necessity of
taking note of conditions naturally enough overlooked
in the first essays at interpretation. Such a nomenclature serves a double purpose: it becomes a record of the
degree of progress actually achieved, and it supplies a
frame-work or scaffolding from which the builders may
carry up the structure to higher elevations. I say a "scaffolding," because it must ever be borne in mind that in
Political Economy, as in all the positive sciences, classification, definition, nomenclature, *is* scaffolding and *not*
foundation—consequently a part of the work which we
must always be prepared to modify or cast aside so soon
as it is found to interfere with the progress of the building.

I remarked just now that Ricardo has given few defi-

nitions, but undoubtedly he carried the science to a point
at which definitions became urgently needed. This want
his successors have attempted to supply, not always, I
think, with a just apprehension of what the aim of definition in a progressive science should be. I am far from
thinking that Political Economy has yet reached a stage
at which a complete nomenclature—a nomenclature making any pretensions to being definitive—could be constructed, or that it would be wise to make the attempt;
but perhaps we have attained a point at which some precision may be usefully essayed in giving shape to its
more fundamental conceptions. Even here, however, it
must be admitted, the science is far yet from having
spoken its last word; and consequently even here our
definitions must still be taken as provisional only—as
liable to be modified, or, it may be, entirely set aside, as
the exigencies of advancing knowledge may prescribe.

§ 3. In connection with the subject of classification, a
further remark must be made. In controversies about
definitions, nothing is more common than to meet objections founded on the assumption that the attribute on
which a definition turns ought to be one which does not
admit of degrees. This being assumed, the objector
goes on to show that the facts or objects placed within
the boundary-line of some definition to which exception
is taken, can not in their extreme instances be clearly
discriminated from those which lie without. Some equivocal example is then taken, and the framer of the definition is challenged to say in which category it is to be
placed. Now it seems to me that an objection of this
kind ignores the inevitable conditions under which a

scientific nomenclature is constructed alike in Political Economy and in all the positive sciences. In such sciences nomenclature, and therefore definition, is based upon classification, and to admit of degrees is the character of all natural facts. As has been said, there are no hard lines in nature. Between the animal and vegetable kingdoms, for example, where is the line to be drawn? Vegetables only, it is true, decompose carbonic acid, but then all vegetables (*e. g.*, the fungi, which obtain their carbon by feeding on other vegetables, and some parasitic plants) do not do so. Some vegetables have motor-action like animals; and, again, the lowest classes of animals have no muscles or nerves. "If, then," says Mr. Murphy, "vegetables have motor-actions like animals, and if there are whole tribes of vegetables which, like animals, do not decompose carbonic acid, and if the lowest class of animals have no muscles or nerves, what is the distinction between the kingdoms? I reply that I do not believe there is any absolute or certain distinction whatever."[1] External objects and events shade off into each other by imperceptible differences, and consequently definitions whose aim it is to classify such objects and events must of necessity be founded on circumstances partaking of this character. The objection proceeds on the assumption that groups exist in nature as clearly discriminated from each other as are the mental ideas formulated by our definitions; so that, where a definition is sound, the boundary of the definition will have its counterpart in external facts. But this is an illusion. No such clearly cut divisions exist in the actual

---

[1] "Habit and Intelligence," by J. J. Murphy, vol. i. p. 163.

universe; and if we feign them in our classifications, we should bear in mind that they are, after all, but fictions —contrivances called for, indeed, and rendered necessary by the weakness of the human intellect, which is unable to contemplate and grasp nature as a whole, but having no counterpart in the reality of things. Let me not, however, be misunderstood. I say our classifications are fictions, but, if sound, they are fictions founded upon fact. The distinctions, formulated in the definition of the class, have a real existence, though the facts or objects lying on each side of the line, and embodying the distinguished attributes, fade into each other by imperceptible degrees. The element of fiction lies, not in the qualities attributed to the things defined, but in the supposition that the objects possessing these qualities are in nature clearly discriminated from those that are without them. It is, therefore, no valid objection to a classification, nor, consequently, to the definition founded upon it, that instances may be found which fall or seem to fall on our lines of demarkation. This is inevitable in the nature of things. But, this notwithstanding, the classification (and therefore the definition) is a good one if, in those instances which do *not* fall on the line, the distinctions marked by the definition are such as it is important to mark—such that the recognition of them will help the inquirer forward toward the desiderated goal.

§ 4. The other portion of the defining process is naming, which, though less important than classification, is still far from being without serious bearing on the successful cultivation of positive knowledge. On this subject the following weighty aphorism, laid down by Mr. Mill, deserves our consideration:

"Whenever the nature of the subject permits our reasoning processes to be, without danger, carried on mechanically, the language should be constructed on as mechanical principles as possible; while, in the contrary case, it should be so constructed that there shall be the greatest possible obstacles to a merely mechanical use of it."[1]

Now within which of the categories here indicated ought Political Economy, regard being had to the nature of its subject, to be considered as falling? Within the category in which our reasoning processes may be carried on mechanically without danger, and in which, therefore, the language should be constructed on as mechanical principles as possible; or within that in which the language should be constructed on the opposite principle of preventing its employment, as far as possible, in a merely mechanical way? I have no hesitation in saying that Political Economy belongs pre-eminently to the group of studies in which the reasoning processes can not be carried on mechanically without the gravest danger, and in which, consequently, the rule laid down in the latter portion of the aphorism just quoted for the construction of a nomenclature ought to be observed. The subject has been discussed by Mr. Mill in its widest bearings in his chapter on the requisites of a philosophical language,[2] and need not therefore be entered into here at any length. But if any one doubt the soundness of this position, I would ask him to reflect upon the mental processes by which economic truths are estab-

---

[1] "Logic," book iv. chap. vi. § 6.   [2] Ibid., book iv. chap. vi.

lished. Let him follow the course of proof in any actual case, and I think he will find that, in order to the
right conduct of the ratiocination, by much the most important condition is that in each step of the argument
the reasoner should keep as fully as possible before him
the actual concrete circumstances denoted by the terms
he employs. I think he will find that it is mainly in
proportion as this has been done that economic reasoning has issued in results of any real value, while to the
failure to satisfy this condition may be traced no small
proportion of the errors which have marked the course
of economic research. I hold, therefore, that it is of the
utmost importance, not only in Political Economy, but in
all social investigation, that the terms of our nomenclature should, as far as possible, serve as constant remind-
ers of the nature of the concrete objects which they are
employed to denote; and that for this purpose, to borrow Mr. Mill's language, "as much meaning as possible
should be thrown into the formation" of our economic
terms, "the aids of derivation and analogy being employed to keep alive a consciousness of all that is signi-
fied by them."

It will serve to throw light at once on the resources
at the disposal of the economist in this respect, and also
on the special difficulties under which Political Economy labors in the matter of definition, if we advert for
a moment to the case of the physical science which
offers the most perfect example of a nomenclature
framed on the principle we have now in view. This
is chemistry, in which the nomenclature is at once
significant and technical—significant, inasmuch as its
terms are composed of elements taken either from ex-

isting or from ancient languages which carry their original meaning into their new occupation; and technical, inasmuch as in their actual form they are only
employed as members of a scientific nomenclature.
Such words as oxygen, hydrogen, carbonate of lime,
peroxide of iron, are all full of meaning, but are never
employed except to express certain known chemical
elements or combinations. From this union of the two
qualities of significance and technicality in its nomenclature an immense advantage results for chemical science; since its terms have in consequence the power
of calling up with great distinctness the concrete objects they are intended to denote; while, having been
constructed for the special purpose of designating those
objects, and never being employed in common speech,
they are free from all associations which could confuse
or mislead either those who employ or those who hear
them. The point, then, to be considered is how far it
is possible to construct for Political Economy a nomenclature which shall fulfill the same ends as nomenclature in chemistry. It appears to me that a certain approximation toward this result is feasible, but only an
approximation; and that, after all is done, the technical
language of Political Economy must ever fall vastly
short of the perfection attained by terminology in
chemical science. In coming to this conclusion, I assume it as settled that the technical terms of Political
Economy are to be taken from popular language, and
this, not merely as regards their elements, as is done
in chemistry, but, so to speak, bodily in their complete
forms. Whether it would, at any time, have been possible to have constructed an economic nomenclature on

the plan adopted in chemistry is perhaps scarcely worth considering. The science has, in fact, been developed through the instrumentality of popular language. It is through this medium that the ideas of all its greatest thinkers have been put forth; it is in this clothing that the world is familiar with them; and it is, therefore, now palpably too late, even if there were no other restraining consideration, to think of recasting its doctrines in other forms. Such words as production, distribution, exchange, value, cost, labor, abstinence, capital, profit, interest, wages, must now for good or for evil remain portions of economic nomenclature; and these have all been drawn in their actual forms from the vernacular, and are in constant use in popular speech. With regard to such words, they are capable enough of fulfilling the first of the two functions fulfilled by nomenclature in chemistry — of calling up, that is to say — always supposing them to be used with deliberation — concrete facts and objects with sufficient vividness. The hitch occurs in their inaptitude for the second of the two purposes required of them, for bringing to the mind the exact facts and objects, neither more nor fewer, which we desire to indicate.

For the position of things is this: The economist finds it necessary, for the reasons which have been stated above, to arrange the phenomena of wealth in classes on a certain principle—that principle being, in fact, the convenience of his own investigations; and he has to find names for the classes thus constituted in the terms of popular language. But popular language has not been framed to suit the convenience of economic speculation, but with quite other views. Its distinctions and classifications do not always or generally coincide with those which are most important for the elucidation of the economy of wealth; and, even where this correspondence is tolerably close, a term in constant use in ordinary speech inevitably gathers round it a vague aroma of association, sure to suggest in particular contexts ideas which have no proper connection with the purposes of scientific research, and which therefore can not but act as hinderances to the reasoning process. That precision of meaning, accordingly, which is so conspicuous in the nomenclature of chemistry, and in general of the physical sciences, is unattainable in Political Economy. Its nomenclature satisfies, indeed, the condition of having plenty of meaning. With even greater vividness than the nomenclature of chemistry, it is capable of calling up the concrete things denoted by its terms; but for this advantage it pays the heavy price of loss of precision—of vagueness and uncertainty as to the proper limitation to be given to its most important words. The remedy, so far as remedy is possible, seems to be twofold: first, to keep our definitions of economic terms as close to the usages of common speech as the requirements of correct classification will allow. Terms must, indeed, now and then be strained to express meanings and to suffer limitations which in ordinary discourse they do not express or bear, since otherwise the ends of classification would be sacrificed; and it is, therefore, no conclusive objection to an economic definition that it does not accurately coincide with popular use. But it should, nevertheless, be fully recognized that such deviations constitute a demerit in definition, and may become a serious one. The second remedy

against the evil is clearness and distinctness of definition wherever terms of importance are employed ; care
being taken, where the economic sense differs from the
popular one, to bring into as strong relief as possible the
points of difference; with which precaution the practice may be usefully combined of throwing in a caveat
from time to time, where the context would be in danger of suggesting the popular rather than the scientific
sense.

§ 5. We may now sum up the general results of the
foregoing discussion :

1. The first requisite of a good definition in Political
Economy is that it should mark those distinctions in
facts and objects which it is important to mark with a
view to the elucidation of the phenomena of wealth ;
and our nomenclature will be good or bad, helpful or
obstructive, according as it coincides with such real and
pertinent distinctions, or sets up others which are arbitrary, fanciful, or irrelevant.

2. So far as is consistent with satisfying the foregoing condition, economic terms should be used as nearly
as possible in their popular sense ; though, as strict ad-
herence to popular usage is not compatible with fulfilling the requirements of sound classification, the mere
circumstance of deviation from popular usage is no conclusive objection to an economic definition.

3. It is no valid objection to an economic definition
that the attribute on which it turns is found to exhibit
degrees in its concrete embodiments. This is inevitable
from the nature of the case.

4. Definitions in the present state of economic science

should be regarded as provisional only, and may be expected to need constant revision and modification with the progress of economic knowledge. Economic definitions are thus progressive. A complete nomenclature pretending to be definitive would at present be premature, and, if framed and generally accepted, would probably prove obstructive. But the time has come when increased precision may be usefully given to the more fundamental conceptions, always with the understanding that these also must still be taken as provisional.

LECTURE VII.

OF THE MALTHUSIAN DOCTRINE OF POPULATION.

§ 1. I ALLUDED in the opening lecture of this course to the present unsettled and unsatisfactory condition of Political Economy with regard to some of its fundamental principles, attributing this state of things, as you will probably remember, to the loose and unscientific views which prevail respecting the character of economic doctrines, and the kind of proof by which they are to be sustained or refuted. This led me in the succeeding lectures to explain and illustrate at some length the character and method of the science. I now propose to vindicate the importance of the topics on which I have been insisting, by showing, in the instance of some fundamental doctrines, the manner in which unscientific views regarding the nature and method of the science have operated in producing those differences of opinion to which I have referred.

One of these doctrines, as I conceive quite fundamental in the science of Political Economy, though impugned and controverted in several recent publications, is the doctrine of population as propounded by Malthus. It would of course be quite impossible, within the compass of a single lecture, to notice, much less satisfactorily to answer, all the various objections that have been in times past, or may still be, urged against this doctrine;

and it would be unnecessary were it possible, most of
them having received as full an answer as they deserve
either from Malthus himself or from succeeding writers.
I shall therefore confine myself to those which, either
from their novelty, or from the circumstance that they
have been lately indorsed by some economists of position, or from their logical character, will be most suitable to the object which I have in view—the illustration
of economic method.

In order, however, that you should appreciate the force
of these objections, it will be necessary for me to state
the doctrine against which they have been advanced.

The celebrated Malthusian doctrine is to the following effect, viz., that there is a "constant tendency in all
animated life to increase beyond the nourishment prepared for it;" or, with reference more particularly to
the human race, that "population tends to increase faster
than subsistence." From what I have already said of
the character of an economic law, as well as from the
terms of the proposition itself, you will at once perceive
that it is not here asserted that population *in fact* increases faster than subsistence : this would of course be
physically impossible. You will also perceive that it is
not inconsistent with this doctrine that subsistence should
in fact be increased much faster than population. It
may also, perhaps, be worth remarking that the doctrine,
as it is stated by Malthus, is not invulnerable to verbal
criticism. The sentence, "population tends to increase
faster than subsistence," is elliptical, and the natural
way of supplying the ellipsis would be by reading it
thus : "Population tends to increase faster than subsistence tends to increase ;" but it can not with propriety be

said that subsistence "tends to increase" at all. I mention this verbal inaccuracy, not because I think it is likely that any candid or intelligent reader could be misled by it, but because I have seen it dwelt upon by anti-Malthusian writers. But, waiving verbal cavils, what Malthus asserted, and what it is the object of his essay to prove, is this—that, regard being had to the powers and propensities in human nature on which the increase of the species depends, there is a constant tendency in human beings to multiply faster than, regard being had to the actual circumstances of the external world, and the power which man can exercise over the resources at his disposal, the means of subsistence are capable of being increased.

The reasoning by which Malthus established this proposition was as follows: he had first to ascertain the capacity and disposition to increase inherent in mankind—in other words, the natural strength of the principle of population. Now, in order to discover the real character of any given principle, obviously the proper course is to consider that principle as it operates when unimpeded by principles of an opposite tendency. Malthus, accordingly, took an instance in which the external conditions were most favorable to the uncontrolled action of the principle of population. This was the case of new colonies, where a population with all the resources of civilization at their command are brought into contact with a new and virgin soil. In these he found that population from internal sources alone, and excluding immigration, frequently doubled itself in twenty-five years.[1] This rate of increase was evidently not owing

---

[1] As a specimen of the intelligence exhibited in criticisms of Malthus, take the following from Blanqui's "Histoire de l'Économie Politique:"

to any thing peculiar or abnormal in the physical or
mental constitution of the inhabitants of such countries,
but owing to the favorable character of the external circumstances under which the principle of population
came into play. He therefore concluded that the ratio
of increase, according to which population doubles itself
in twenty-five years, represents the natural force of the
principle—the rate at which population always *tends* to
increase—the rate at which, if unrestrained by principles
of an opposite character or by the physical incapacity of
sustaining life, population always will increase.

On the other hand, on looking to the means placed at
man's disposal for obtaining subsistence, Malthus found
that it was physically impossible that subsistence could
be increased at this rate. The surface of the globe is
limited; the portions of it suitable to cultivation and ac-
cessible to human enterprise are still more limited; and
the difficulty of obtaining food from a limited area increases as the quantity raised from it is increased.[1] If,

---

"Le choix que Malthus a fait de l'Amérique, où la population double tous
les vingt-cinq ans, n'est pas plus concluant que celui de la Suède, où, se-
lon M. Godwin, elle ne double que tous les cent ans. Les sociétés ne pro-
cèdent point ainsi par périodes regulières, comme les astres et les saisons,
etc." Malthus could find his opponents in arguments, but not in brains.

[1] Against this it is urged that, however true the statement may be as an
abstract proposition, yet, regard being had to the actual state of the world
—the increased supplies of food which even the most advanced countries
under an improved agricultural system are capable of yielding, as well as
the vast districts in America, New Zealand, and elsewhere, which are yet
to be brought under cultivation—the doctrine must, for ages to come, be
destitute of all practical significance. In a review of Mansfield's "Para-
guay, Brazil, and the Platte," in *Fraser's Magazine* (Nov., 1856), the
writer, after rather more than the usual misrepresentation of Malthusian views, puts the objection thus:

"Meanwhile stood by, laughing bitterly enough, the really practical
men—men such as the author of the book now before us: the travelers,

e. g., 40,000,000 quarters of corn are produced annually in the United Kingdom at present, it might be possible

---

the geographers, the experimental men of science, who took the trouble, before deciding on what could be, to find out what was, and, as it were, 'took stock' of the earth and her capabilities before dogmatizing on the future fate of her inhabitants. And, 'What?' they asked, in blank astonishment, 'what, in the name of maps and common-sense, means this loud squabble? What right has any one to dogmatize on the future of humanity while the far greater part of the globe is yet unredeemed from the wild beast and the wild hunter? If scientific agriculture be too costly, is there not room enough on the earth for as much unscientific and cheap tillage as would support many times over her present population? What matters it, save as a question of temporary make-shift, whether England can be made to give thirty-three bushels of wheat per acre instead of thirty-one, by some questionably remunerative outlay of capital, while the Texan squatter, without any capital save his own two hands, is growing eighty bushels an acre? Your disquisitions about the "margin of productiveness" are interesting, curious, probably correct, valuable in old countries, but nowhere else. For is the question whether men shall live, or even be born at all, to be settled by them, forsooth, while the Valley of the Ottawa can grow corn enough to supply all England, the Valley of the Mississippi for all Europe?—while Australia is a forest, instead of being, as it will be one day, the vineyard of the world?—while New Zealand and the Falklands are still waste; and Polynesia, which may become the Greece of the New World, is worse than waste?—while Nebraska alone is capable of supporting a population equal to France and Spain together?—while, in the Old World, Asia Minor, once the garden of old Rome, lies a desert in the foul and lazy hands of the Ottoman?—while the tropics produce almost spontaneously a hundred valuable articles of food, all but overlooked as yet in the exclusive cultivation of cotton and sugar? and, finally (asks Mr. Mansfield in his book), while South America alone contains a territory of some eight hundred millions of square miles, at least equaling Egypt in climate, and surpassing England in fertility; easy of access; provided, by means of its great rivers, with unrivaled natural means of communication, and "with water-power enough to turn all the mills in the world;" and needing nothing but men to make it one of the gardens of the world?'"

There are travelers and travelers. The passage just quoted gives us the view of one class on the problem raised by Malthus; on the other hand, Von Humboldt, in his "Essay on New Spain" (vol. i. p. 107), characterizes the work of Malthus as "one of the most profound works on Political Economy which has ever appeared." But to come to the reviewer's argument:

at the end of twenty-five years, by means of improved agricultural processes, to raise 80,000,000 quarters annu-

The objection, it will be observed, is a purely practical one. It is not denied that "population tends to increase faster than subsistence;" that, however great be the quantity of food which the earth is capable of yielding, population may ultimately overtake it, and tends to do so; but it is said, of what practical moment is this to us living now, with the boundless resources of new worlds still at our disposal? The answer—the *practical* answer—is, it is every thing to us, if these resources, however extensive, are not *in fact* turned to account. It matters not whether the obstacles be physical or moral, whether absolute and insuperable or the result simply of prejudice and ignorance, so long as they are effectual in preventing the cultivation of the countries in question. So long as this is the case, these countries, to all *practical* intents and purposes, may be said not to exist for us: they can no more be counted on as means of supporting population than the countries in the moon. Yet because, forsooth, "the Valley of the Ottawa *can* grow corn enough to support all England," although it is admitted that it *does* not do so, and it is not asserted that there is any immediate prospect that it *will*, this "really practical" reviewer holds that it is the height of absurdity to speak of the necessity of restraining population, and treats all those who do as dreamers and lunatics!

A laborer, *e. g.*, in Dorsetshire, on nine shillings a week is hesitating about marriage. The "speculative" Malthusian advises him to wait a little while till he saves enough to form at least the nucleus of a support for his wife and family. "The really practical man," on the other hand, says to him, Why hesitate? Is not the Valley of the Ottawa capable of growing food for all England?

The immense food-producing capabilities of the earth yet available for us were not overlooked by Malthus, nor, so far as I know, have they been by those who accept his doctrine, nor is there any reason to suppose that either master or followers have underrated the importance of turning these capabilities to account. They have, however, urged that the existence of capabilities is no reason for weakening the restraints on population; because, whatever be the extent of these resources, the development of them must be a work of time, and population is found in fact to be always fully able to keep pace with the process. The instinct which holds people to their native land, in spite of the alluring prospects of other regions, the tardiness with which capital moves to new countries, and the ignorance, indolence, and barbarism of most of the races which occupy them, render the introduction of systematized industry into such regions a mattre of much difficulty and of slow accomplishment. The greater part of India has now been under English rule for a century, and yet we know how difficult it is to attract capital thither without a government guarantee;

ally: it is perhaps conceivable that, by forcing to the highest degree every patch of cultivable land in the kingdom, at the end of fifty years 160,000,000 quarters might be raised: certain, however, it is that the annual production of corn in the United Kingdom could not go on forever at this rate; but it is no less certain, in view of the capacity of increase in human beings, that the population of the United Kingdom *could*, and, in view of their natural propensities in the same direction, that they *would*, proceed at this rate forever, till brought to a stop by the physical impossibility of obtaining food—supposing, that is to say, that their natural power and disposition to multiply operated unchecked by principles of an opposite character.

The result, therefore, of the consideration of these facts by Malthus was the enunciation of the doctrine

---

and, notwithstanding all that has been written and spoken of the boundless resources of India, and the pressing needs of England for articles to the production of which her soil and climate are peculiarly suitable, how little has yet been done to turn these advantages to account! What would a Manchester cotton-spinner think of the advice not to hesitate about erecting new mills and machinery, because, though the supply of cotton be rather short just now, the plains of the Deccan are capable of producing more than he will be able to work up for half a century? Yet the reviewer who, in the somewhat more momentous affair of human existence, gives precisely analogous advice takes credit to himself for pre-eminent practical wisdom.

With regard to the other point adverted to, the possibility of largely increasing the quantity of subsistence raised even in old countries, similar considerations apply. The fact is undoubtedly true ; but more food is nevertheless not raised. If it be asked why this is so, the answer is, because, while agricultural skill remains at its present point, an increased production of food would necessitate a fall in farmers' profits. And if it be further asked as to the grounds of this necessity, the inquirer may be referred to "the diminishing productiveness of the soil" — the impenetrable barrier against which all anti-Malthusian plans and arguments are ultimately shivered.

which I have just stated—that there is in human beings a tendency to multiply faster than subsistence ; to
increase faster than subsistence is capable of being increased.   Population, however, as I have said, whatever
might be its tendency, could not increase faster than
subsistence, inasmuch as human beings can not live
without food ; and further investigation showed that
subsistence in most countries, and in all improving
countries, had in fact increased faster than population.
Malthus therefore turned his attention to the discovery
of those antagonizing principles which keep in check
the natural power of population.   These, he found,
were reducible to two classes, which he designated the
preventive and positive checks.   The preventive checks
included all causes which operated in restraining the
natural power or disposition of mankind to increase
their numbers, and were generally comprised under the
two heads of prudence with regard to marriage, and
vice, so far as it interfered with fecundity.   The positive checks included those causes of premature death
incident to a redundant population, of which the principal were insufficient food, famine, disease, and war.

§ 2. Such, in outline, is the doctrine of Malthus ; and
such the line of reasoning by which it was established.
As to its importance, it is scarcely too much to say that,
while throwing a strong light on not a few of the dark-
est passages of history, it in a short time revolutionized
the current modes of thinking on social and industrial
problems.   The material well-being of a community
mainly depends on the proportion which exists between
the quantity of necessaries and comforts in that com-

munity and the number of persons among whom these are divided, of which necessaries and comforts by far the most important item is food. All plans, therefore, for improving the condition of the masses of mankind, in order to be effectual, must be directed to an alteration in this proportion, and, to be permanent, must aim at making this alteration permanent. Now, Malthus showed that the strength of the principle of population is such that, if allowed to operate unrestrained, no possible increase of food could keep pace with it. It consequently followed that, in order to the permanent improvement of the masses of mankind, the development of principles which should impose some restraint on the natural tendency of the principle of population was indispensable ; and that, however an increase in the productiveness of industry might for a time improve the condition of a community, yet this alone, if unaccompanied by the formation of habits of self-control and providence on the part of the people themselves, could not be relied upon as an ultimate safeguard against distress.

The same discovery [1] of Malthus—in his own lan-

---

[1] I say "discovery," because, although it is true that the fundamental fact on which Malthus's doctrine rested had frequently been noticed before (*vide*, for example, McPherson's "Annals of Commerce," 1590, where he quotes a passage from a work by a Piedmontese Jesuit, Botero, "On the Causes of the Greatness of Cities," in which the writer puts the question—" What is the reason that cities, once grown to greatness, increase not onward according to that proportion ?" and gives the Malthusian answer), its bearing and importance with reference to the interests of mankind were all but wholly unappreciated until Malthus wrote. He it was who first called attention to the vast consequences involved in a fact patent to every observer, and occasionally taken notice of in particular instances, but never before understood in its full significance. And this, I may observe, is the nature of almost all discoveries in the region of social

guage, " the constant pressure of population against subsistence "—gave the key to many social and historic problems : disclosed, for example, the latent cause by virtue of which the world has been peopled ; which forced the shepherds of Asia from the primitive birth-place of the human race ; which led the Greeks to throw off numerous colonies ; which compelled the great migrations of the northern barbarians ; and which is now sending successive swarms of emigrants to carry the English race and language to the utmost corners of the earth.

Armed with the same principle, Malthus was enabled to give a complete and philosophic answer to the communistic plans which were at that time ardently advocated by Godwin, Owen, and others, by showing that, as such schemes offered no inducement to the exercise of prudential restraint, and removed those which already existed, they were defective just in that point without which human improvement was impossible : they provided no security against a redundant population — none, therefore, against the want and misery which a redundant population must occasion.

The practical lessons which Malthus deduced from the law of population were no less important. Up to the time when the essay on population was written the prevailing opinion among statesmen of all shades of politics was that a dense population was the surest

---

inquiry, as well as to some extent also in the sciences of organic nature. For example, the facts which form the basis of the Darwinian doctrine of species had not only been often noticed before, but, as Mr. Darwin shows, had been systematically acted on by breeders and others—in fact, made the basis of an art. No one, however, will say that this detracted from the originality of Darwin's discovery.

proof of national prosperity, and the encouragement of population the first duty of a statesman. As the gentle humorist put it, the honest man who married early and brought up a large family was thought to do more real service than he who continued single and only talked of population. Under the influence of this delusion, colonization[1] was discouraged, as tending to depopulate the mother country, while the poor-laws, over and above their indirect influence in undermining individual providence, placed a direct premium upon multiplication; and in general every plan for the improvement of society was approved and supported just in proportion to its supposed influence in augmenting the numbers of the people. The reasonings of Malthus went, as I have explained, to establish a conclusion directly opposite to this—to show that, as regards the number of a people, the danger lay on the side, not of deficiency, but of excess; and that, therefore, plans of social improvement were to be approved, not in proportion as they tended to encourage the increase of population, but in proportion as they tended to develop those qualities of self control and providence on which its restriction within due limits depends.[2]

---

[1] "Emigration," says Doctor Johnson, "is hurtful to human happiness, for it spreads mankind." Dean Tucker, one of the few Englishmen who, during the American War of Independence, favored separation, did so expressly on the ground that it would check emigration. See his "Tracts," p. 206.

[2] It by no means follows from any thing that has been said above that paucity of population or the slowness of its advances is to be taken as a proof of national prosperity; or, *vice versâ*, that a numerous or rapidly increasing population is inconsistent therewith, as is almost invariably asserted or implied by anti-Malthusian writers. Mr. Rickards, *e. g.*, says: "Mr. Malthus and the disciples of his school unite in representing the

Such were some of the consequences which resulted in social and political theory and practice from the great

---

supposed pressure of population against food *as increasing in intensity in direct proportion to the populousness of a community;*" and, after giving the number of inhabitants to the square mile in some of the principal countries in the world, the result of the comparison being to show the greatest density of population in England, he adds, " England, therefore, is the country in which, *according to the theory in question*, the pressure of over-population ought to be most severe."—" Population and Capital," pp. 117, 118.

It is evident that the theory in question involves no such consequence, referring, as it does, to the *relation* subsisting between population and food, and asserting nothing whatever respecting the absolute amount of either. The statement, however, is not simply an unwarrantable inference : it amounts to a direct misrepresentation of Malthus, since it imputes to him an opinion which he has in terms disavowed—*e. g.*, " *It is an utter misconception of my argument to infer that I am an enemy to population.* I am only an enemy to vice and misery, and consequently to that unfavorable proportion between population and food which produces these evils. *But this unfavorable proportion has no necessary connection with the quantity of absolute population* which a country may contain. On the contrary, *it is more frequently found in countries which are very thinly peopled than in those which are more populous.* . . . *In the desirableness of a great and efficient population, I do not differ from the warmest advocates of increase.* I am perfectly ready to acknowledge, with the writers of old, that it is not extent of territory, but extent of population, that measures the power of states. It is only as to the mode of obtaining a vigorous and efficient population that I differ from them, and in thus differing I conceive myself entirely borne out by experience, that great test of all human speculations."

The practical difference in the results to which Malthusian and anti-Malthusian views lead may be made clearer by considering how they would apply in a given case.

The stationary state of population in France, which has lately been made the subject of much remark, would probably be regarded by both schools as indicating something amiss in the social condition of that country ; but while the anti-Malthusian would regard it as the source of the disease, the Malthusian would consider it as merely a symptom, and a symptom, as far as it went, alleviative of the disorder. According to the views of the former, the proper cure for the social malady would be to encourage population by offering premiums for large families, or by throwing the responsibility of providing for them on the state. I do not say that any one now would seriously recommend this policy, but I say it is a legitimate work of Malthus. It appears to me that, in following the course which led him to the result he reached, Malthus followed the only course by which important economic truths are to be discovered. You will observe, his method was strictly in conformity with that which I have been recommending in these lectures as the scientific method of Political Economy. He commenced by considering the nature and force of a known principle of human nature: he took account of the actual external conditions under which it came into operation; he traced the consequences which would result supposing it to operate unrestrained under these ascertained conditions; he then inquired how far in fact the principle had been restrained; and, lastly, investigated the nature of the antagonizing agencies through the operation of

---

consequence from anti-Malthusian doctrines; it was universally accepted as such, and acted on as such, up to the close of the last century; and if the same policy is not still openly advocated, it is owing to the influence which the writings of Malthus have exercised even among those who affect to repudiate his teaching.

On the other hand, the Malthusian would regard the stationariness of population in France as an alleviative symptom of the social malady. That population does not advance is, indeed, in itself (apart from other considerations) an evil—it implies, at all events, a certain negation of human happiness; but it is better that population should not advance than that it should advance in increasing pauperism and wretchedness. The Malthusian, therefore, would consider how the material resources of France might be expanded, and her means of supporting population increased; but he would carefully abstain from encouraging population, because he would know that, owing to the natural strength of the principle, however great might be the expansion of her resources, population would advance *at least as fast as was desirable.* On the contrary, he would take care, while endeavoring to augment her means, not to weaken, but rather to strengthen, those prudential habits which at present exist. No possible immediate gain, if obtained by a relaxation in this respect, would be considered by him as an adequate compensation for the future evils which such relaxation would entail.

H

which tne restraint was effected. By these means he arrived at the ultimate causes in the principles of human nature, and the facts of the external world on which the condition of the mass of mankind in the matter of subsistence depends, and furnished for the first time the solution of an important problem in the laws of the distribution of wealth.

§ 3. So much, then, for the doctrine of Malthus; and now for his opponents. One of the most prominent of the writers who have recently taken the field against him is Mr. Rickards, late Professor of Political Economy at Oxford. Of his work on " Population and Capital " the chief portion is devoted to an elaborate attack on the position of Malthus. The objections advanced by Mr. Rickards are not absolutely new,[1] but they are stated by him with greater fullness and clearness than I have seen them elsewhere, and I shall, therefore, avail myself of his statement of them. The following passage is taken from the work just referred to:

" It is obvious that there are two methods by which the respective rates of increase of man and of subsistence may be compared. They may be regarded—I mean, of course, both the one and the other—either in the abstract or in the concrete ; either potentially or practically. We may investigate, for instance, according to the laws of nature manifested by experience, what is the stated period within which a given society of human beings are physically capable of doubling their numbers, abstracting the operation of those checks that impaired longevity and increased mor-

---

[1] See Lawson's " Lectures on Political Economy ;" also Laing's " Travels in Europe," chap. iii.

tality which may be found practically keeping down the number of any society. On the other hand, we may estimate the potential rate of increase of those animals or substances which are adapted for human subsistence, assuming no obstacle to their multiplication to arise from the difficulty of finding hands to rear or space upon the earth to nourish them. By this method we may ascertain which of the two elements, population or subsistence, is physically capable of the greater expansion in a given time. Or we may adopt another mode of testing their relative rates of increase—we may compare the progress of man and of production in the actual state of any community, or of all communities together. In all existing societies there are checks in operation upon the multiplication of the human species. There are checks, likewise, upon the indefinite increase of the animal and vegetable world. We may take the operation of the checks into account on both sides of our calculation. In any given country, or in the world at large, if we like it better, we may compute, with reference to the actual state of things—looking to the experience of the past, and to the circumstances of the present, to all the causes, social, moral, or political, which restrain the propagation both of man and of his food—what has actually been, or what probably may be henceforward, the comparative rates of increase of population and of production. Either of these two methods of comparison would be fair and logical. I need scarcely add that the latter will be more likely to conduce to a useful practical conclusion. But a third method, which can not fail to lead us by the road of false logic to an utterly wrong result, is that of comparing the potential increase of mankind, according to the unchecked laws of nature, with the actual progress in any given country of production, excluding the operation of the counteracting forces on the one side, importing them into the estimate on the other. It is no wonder, when we use such a balance as this, if the scales are found to hang prodigiously unequal. . . .

" But it requires nothing more than a careful attention

to this point to bring out in a clear point of view the fundamental fallacy of the whole argument. What is that ratio in regard to the multiplication of *subsistence* which Mr. Malthus has placed in contrast with the *potential* increase of human beings? *Not* the potential increase of animal and vegetable existences proper for the food of men under the like favorable conditions; 'the power left to exert itself with perfect freedom,' limited by no check or obstacle, which formed his datum in regard to population. He enters into no estimate as to the periods in which, according to the laws of nature, the fruits of the earth, the corn, the olive, and the vine, are capable—it is vain to talk of *duplication* in such cases, but—of multiplication, some thirtyfold, some sixtyfold, some a hundredfold. He omits to consider the almost marvelous fecundity of some of those animals which form, in civilized communities, the chief subsistence of the mass of the people. . . . His calculation as to the ratio in which subsistence may be multiplied is founded upon the state of things then actually existing in England. He compares the abstract with the concrete —nature, in the region of hypothesis, acting in 'perfect freedom,' with nature obstructed by all the 'checks' which restrain production in the actual world."[1]

The first point to be remarked upon in this is that Mr. Rickards does not here deny the doctrine of Malthus in the sense in which Malthus asserted that doctrine—he admits that in *this* sense "the scales" *do* "hang prodigiously unequal;" nor does he impugn the reasoning by which Malthus deduced from the doctrine *thus understood* the conclusions which it was the object of his essay to establish: in short, he neither denies the premises of the Malthusian argument, nor their sufficiency to establish the Malthusian conclusion. The passage, there-

---

[1] "Population and Capital," pp. 68–70, 73, 75.

fore, which I have quoted, if it be intended as any thing more than a verbal criticism on the form in which the meaning of Malthus is expressed, must be regarded as an example of the fallacy called *ignoratio elenchi;* and if my object were simply to defend the Malthusian doctrine, I might at once pass by these objections as irrelevant. As an example, however, of the confused notions which prevail respecting economic method, it will be desirable to consider them somewhat more at length.

I propose, therefore, to show that, while the comparison instituted by Malthus is perfectly legitimate and logical, those suggested by Mr. Rickards are wholly irrelevant to the ends of economic science, inasmuch as, whether concluded in the affirmative or negative, they illustrate no economic principle whatever, and afford us no assistance in solving any problem presented by the phenomena of wealth.

And here I may remark in passing that, granting for the moment that a comparison of the abstract with the concrete be inadmissible, the criticism may be at once obviated by substituting for the word "subsistence" the expression "capacity of the soil to yield subsistence," which equally well conveys the meaning of Malthus. We may then compare the abstract with the abstract, the "potential fecundity" of man with the "potential" fertility of the soil; and we may deduce from the proposition thus stated precisely the same conclusions which it was the object of Malthus to inculcate.[1]

---

[1] Mr. Rickards, in fact, elsewhere states the question in this way: "Now, precisely the same assumption—that of the diminishing productiveness of the land as compared with the *undiminished* power of human fecundity—forms the basis of the Malthusian theory."—" Population and Capital," p. 127.

But why, let us ask, should a comparison of the abstract with the concrete be necessarily illogical ? I know of no criterion by which to decide on the propriety of a comparison except by reference to the object for which the comparison is instituted. The object which Malthus had in view in writing his essay was to ascertain the influence of the principle of population upon human well-being;[1] to ascertain whether the natural force of the principle was such that, with a view to the happiness of mankind, it should be stimulated or restrained ; whether it was desirable that inducements should be held out tending to encourage early marriages and large families ; or, on the contrary, whether we should favor those institutions and usages of society of which the tendency is to develop the virtues of prudence and moral restraint in the relations of the sexes. This was clearly and properly an economic question—it was a question as to the influence of a given principle on the distribution of wealth ; and it was one which, from the terms in which it is stated, evidently involved the very comparison to which Mr. Rickards objects—a comparison of the natural and inherent force of the principle of population with the actual means at man's disposal, situated as he is in the world, for obtaining subsistence — a comparison of " nature in the region of hypothesis, acting with perfect freedom, with nature obstructed by all the checks which

---

[1] " To enter fully into this question, and to enumerate all the causes that have hitherto influenced human improvement, would be much beyond the power of an individual. The principal object of the present essay is to examine the effects of one great cause intimately united with the very nature of man ; which, though it has been constantly and powerfully operating since the commencement of society, has been little noticed by writers who have treated this subject."—Malthus, " Essay on Population," p. 2. ed. 1807.

restrain production in the actual world." Mr. Rickards, therefore, either must maintain that the problem which Malthus proposed to solve—the influence of the principle of population upon human well-being—upon the distribution of wealth—was not a legitimate problem, or he must admit that a comparison of the abstract with the concrete is not an improper comparison.

Indeed, if the consideration of the tendency of a given principle — its "potential" capacity — in connection with the "actual" circumstances under which it comes into operation, is to be proscribed as involving a comparison of the abstract with the concrete, it is difficult to imagine how the complex phenomena of nature are to be investigated, and traced to the various causes producing them.

But, further, I maintain that neither of the comparisons, insisted on by Mr. Rickards as being the only legitimate comparisons, can lead to the discovery of any economic principle whatever, or help us to the solution of any economic problem. The first of the comparisons suggested by Mr. Rickards as that which Malthus might properly have instituted is the comparison of population in the abstract with food in the abstract — the "potential" increase of the one with the "potential" increase of the other—in a word, the comparison of the fecundity of a human pair with the fecundity of a grain of wheat. Had he instituted this comparison, he would, says Mr. Rickards, have done that which at least "was logical and fair," and, we may safely admit, would have been led to no conclusion that could have disturbed the serenity of the most orthodox philosopher.

There can be no doubt that the capacity of increase in a grain of wheat (the conditions most favorable to its cultivation being assumed) is immeasurably greater than the capacity of increase in mankind (the conditions most favorable to their multiplication being also assumed); inasmuch as while population under the most favorable circumstances takes twenty or twenty-five years to double itself, a grain of wheat in rich soil may yield twenty or thirty or forty fold in a year; and it is quite possible that in a work on the comparative physiology of plants and animals this fact may possess some importance. But the question for a political economist is, what economic principle can be deduced from it? What light does it throw on the class of problems with which he has to deal? Mr. Rickards will perhaps reply — it follows from the comparison that subsistence tends to increase faster than population. Understood in the sense Malthus affixed to the terms, this proposition would represent an important tendency influencing the phenomena of wealth — in other words, an economic law: were it true in this sense that "subsistence tended to increase faster than population," all the inferences which Malthus drew from the opposite principle, and, I may add, most of the doctrines of Political Economy as they are received at present, might be reversed; nay, the most important phenomena of society as it is at present constituted would be inexplicable. But, when understood as Mr. Rickards insists on understanding it, the bearing of the proposition on economic problems is not obvious. Let us test it by actual trial. Assuming, as is undoubtedly the case, that the abstract capacity of increase in a grain of corn is greater than the abstract capacity of increase in a human pair, and that in this sense subsistence tends to increase faster than population — in what manner does the fact here asserted affect human interests in their economic aspects ? What phenomenon of wealth does it explain ? What practical lesson does it afford ? Does it throw any light on the causes on which the progress and physical well-being of society depend ? Does it explain why rent tends to rise and profits to fall as society advances ? Why the English laborer receives less than the American, and more than the Hindû ? Why old countries import raw produce and export manufactured articles, while new countries reverse this process ? Does it explain why, as civilization advances, the condition of the mass of the people generally improves ? Not one of these questions can be completely answered without reference to the doctrine of population as Malthus stated and understood that doctrine ; but if, with Mr. Rickards and those who agree with him, we are to understand the doctrine as expressing a comparison of the tendency to increase in human beings, not with the actual means at their disposal for obtaining subsistence, but with the capacity of increase in the vegetable world under impossible conditions, I can not find that it helps us in any way to the solution of these or any other economic problems.

I defined an economic law (as you will probably remember) as a proposition expressing a tendency deduced from the principles of human nature and external facts, and affecting the production or distribution of wealth. The comparison instituted between population and subsistence by Mr. Rickards certainly expresses a tendency deduced from human nature and external facts, but is wanting in the other condition of an economic law, as I have ventured to define it : it expresses no tendency affecting the production and distribution of wealth. I can not, therefore, see on what ground it is entitled to the place which Mr. Rickards would assign it.

The other comparison suggested by our author as one that might properly be instituted (and to it he appears to attach most importance) is the comparison of " population in the concrete " with " subsistence in the concrete "—the comparison, that is to say, of the progress which has actually taken place in the population of a given district during a given time, with the progress which, in the same district and during the same time, has taken place in subsistence. Now I am far from saying that such a comparison may not bring to light facts of a valuable character—facts which, if duly reflected upon and interpreted by the light of economic science, may lead to important conclusions, and possibly to the discovery of some new economic principle ; but I entirely deny that a proposition, embodying the crude results of this comparison, can be considered as a portion of Political Economy, or that it possesses any of the attributes of an economic law.

It is true, indeed, that the term " law " is frequently applied to mere generalizations of complex phenomena — to propositions which simply express the order in which facts have been observed to occur ; and provided the purely empirical character of such generalizations be borne in mind, there can be no objection to the name. Even in this sense, however, to entitle

a proposition to the character of a "law," some degree
of regularity and uniformity in the observed sequence
is required. Now, with respect to the comparison
which Mr. Rickards proposes to institute between the
relative advances which have taken place in population and subsistence, no such uniformity or regularity
is observable. In some nations subsistence has advanced more rapidly than population; in others population has advanced more rapidly than subsistence; and
in the same nation at different times the results have
been different, population and subsistence taking the
lead by turns. The utmost that can be said with truth
is that, on the whole, as nations advance in civilization,
the proportion generally alters in favor of subsistence
—a proposition which, I think, can scarcely pretend to
the dignity of a "law," even in the loosest sense of that
word.

But even if we were to suppose the relative advance
of population and subsistence to be constant and uniform, and the rate to be well ascertained, I should still
deny that a proposition embodying the results of this
comparison could correctly be called a doctrine of Political Economy; that is to say, I should deny that such
a proposition could with propriety be placed in the
same category of truths with those which assert that
within the range of effective competition normal value
is governed by cost of production; that fluctuations in
value are governed by the conditions of demand and
supply in relation to the particular commodity; that
the rate of profit varies inversely with proportional
wages as understood by Ricardo; that "economic rent"
depends on the difference in the returns of the soil to

different capitals; in a word, with the most important principles of economic science. Each of these propositions expresses some tendency affecting the production and distribution of wealth; they have all been deduced from known principles of human nature and ascertained physical facts; and they are all available in explanation of the phenomena of wealth. But a proposition asserting the results (even supposing these results to be perfectly regular and uniform) of a comparison between population in the concrete and food in the concrete, possesses none of these attributes. It does not express any tendency influencing the phenomena of wealth, but exhibits the composite result and evidence of many tendencies; it is not deduced from the principles of human nature and external facts, but from the statistics of society, or from the crude generalizations of history; and, lastly, it is not a principle helping us to the solution of any of the problems of our complex civilization, but itself presents a complex problem for our solution.

I say that such a comparison will not help us to the solution of any of the problems of our complex civilization; for, granting the fact to be as Mr. Rickards asserts it to be, and as, on the whole, making large allowance for exceptional cases, I believe it is—granting that, as a general rule, the means of subsistence, and we may add the comforts and luxuries of life, have advanced in civilized communities more rapidly than population, what light does this throw either upon the influence of the principle of population on the one hand, or of the causes regulating the production of subsistence on the other— of their influence, I say, upon the progress of society and the phenomena of wealth? All that we are warranted in inferring from the state of things assumed is the predominance *on the whole* in the given circumstances of the causes tending to advance over those tending to retard the social or economic condition of a nation; but it affords no ground for inference respecting the character or inherent strength of any particular cause affecting that condition—such as the principle of population. The fact of the arrival of a vessel in New York is no proof that she had the wind in her favor: she may have had recourse to steam to counteract its effects. The speed at which she travels and the direction of her course do not depend upon the force of the steam impelling, or of the winds assisting, or of the currents thwarting, or of the friction impeding, but is "the last result and joint effect of all." Such, also, is the progress of society. It represents the result of a vast number of forces, physical, intellectual, social, and moral; and it advances or recedes or oscillates as one kind or other prevails. But from the mere consideration of the rough result, the general total, it would be as vain to attempt to deduce the character or tendency of any single cause affecting it — of any given economic principle — as it would be to elicit a theory of the Atlantic currents from the statistics of voyages between Liverpool and New York.

Mr. Rickards, however, holds that the comparison which we have been considering does throw light on the causes of economic phenomena. The actual advance which the various communities have made in material improvement, proves, according to him, "the natural ascendency of the force of production over the force of population." "It can have emanated," he says, "from no other source. The primitive possessors of the earth were destitute of all things. The earth has been the source of all the wealth which has accumulated in the hands of their descendants. . . . If, while the number of cultivators has gone on increasing, this surplus has become greater and greater, and the whole people wealthier, it must follow that production has a tendency to increase more rapidly than population, and that the accumulation of wealth which accompanies the progress of society is attributable to this cause."[1]

In order to the cogency of the argument it is obviously necessary that the terms "force of production" and "force of population" should include *all* the causes influencing the economic progress of society; and in *this* sense to say that the force of production is superior to the force of population is only in other words to say that the causes tending to advance society are on the whole more powerful than the causes tending to retard it; the name "force of production" being given to the one set of causes, and that of "force of population" to the other. It is, in short, a mere reproduction of the fact of progress under another form, but does not advance us a step toward an explanation of that fact which is the problem to be solved. It is as if a person should argue that the fact of a train leaving Dublin and arriving in Belfast proves the ascendency in railways of the "force of locomotion" over the "force of immobility," on the ground that the actual progress of the train could be due to no other cause; and the argument

---

[1] P. 115.

would be valid—a similar assumption being made to that latent in the reasoning I have quoted, namely, that the "force of locomotion" included all the causes propelling the train, and the "force of immobility" all the causes retarding it. The engineer, however, who should make the discovery would scarcely find that he had added much to his stock of useful knowledge.

§ 4. I have now endeavored to show that the comparisons suggested by Mr. Rickards in lieu of that which Malthus instituted, lead to no economic principle whatever, and furnish no aid toward the solution of any problems connected with the phenomena of wealth. In further proof of the entire irrelevancy, with reference to the ends of the science, of Mr. Rickards's exposition of the laws of population, I may add that, having established these laws, apparently to his own satisfaction, he nevertheless does not apply them to the solution of any problems of wealth, nor does he attempt to make them the ground of any practical suggestions; on the contrary, such practical lessons as he does inculcate on the subject of population are directly at variance with his own theoretical conclusions.

You have seen that, while Malthus maintained that population tended to increase faster than subsistence, he held, consistently with this, that the principle of population was a power which it was desirable to restrain, and advocated, as a means to this end, the formation of habits of prudence and self-control. Mr. Rickards, as you have also seen, emphatically denies this doctrine: he maintains, on the contrary, that subsistence tends to increase faster than population—that it does so both in the "abstract" and in the "concrete," both "potentially" and "actually;" and, further, that "production" as compared with "population" is "the greater power of the two." Mr. Rickards having thus given a direct negative to the principle of Malthus, it would be natural to suppose that in the practical treatment of the question he would be equally at variance with him. It would be natural to suppose that, as he maintains that subsistence both "potentially" and "actually" tends to outstrip population, he would be released from all apprehension as to the danger of population outstripping subsistence. If "production" be the "superior power," there seems no reason—provided only men be industrious, provided only the machinery of production be kept in motion — that mankind should not multiply without stay or limit, since, on this hypothesis, it is always competent to them to keep the means of physical comfort in advance of their increase. There seems no reason, in short, that the population of every country in Europe should not advance at the American rate, constantly doubling itself in periods of twenty-five years; or, at least, if there be any reason for restraining population, we should not expect to find it in the difficulty of procuring subsistence. You will, therefore, probably be surprised to find that Mr. Rickards not only recognizes the necessity of placing a restraint on the principle of population, but does so on the express ground of the limits placed by nature on the increase of subsistence.

"Individual prudence," he says,[1] " is the proper check to precipitate marriages; an appeal to the consequences

---

[1] P. 204.

which will recoil on the parties themselves and their innocent offspring is the appropriate and cogent argument to deter them from rash engagements. Let it not be said," he continues, " that in thus arguing I am substituting a principle of selfishness for one of duty. It is not so: prudence is here an obligation of morality."
. . . " Whatever fluctuations," he adds, " may betide the labor market, let each man, in forming his private connections, act with the forethought and discretion that become a responsible being, and society will have no cause of complaint against him, for over-population will be impossible." This is excellent advice. But what are the grounds of it?—why should " over-population " be possible in the absence of forethought and discretion? why should prudence in respect to marriage be an obligation of morality? Simply, Mr. Rickards tells us, quoting the language of M. Say (not to refute, but to adopt it), because " the tendency of men to reproduce their kind, and their means of doing so, are, we may say, infinite; but their means of subsistence are limited."[1]

I must leave Mr. Rickards to reconcile his practical lessons with his theoretical conclusions—his advocacy of a restraint on population on the ground of the limitation of subsistence, with his doctrine that subsistence " potentially " and " actually " tends to increase faster than population. It appears to me that the conclusion is inevitable—either his doctrines, in the sense in which he understands them, are irrelevant to the purposes of Political Economy, or his precepts are in direct contravention of his doctrines.

---

[1] P. 186.

Before concluding, I must notice one more position of Mr. Rickards. In the preface to the work which I have been noticing he puts this dilemma: "If the conclusion of the Essay on Population be true, it seems to me to involve this inevitable consequence — that there has been a miscalculation of means to ends in the arrangements of the universe—either man has been made too prolific, or the earth too sterile."[1] Let us meet this argument frankly. The conclusion of Malthus does undoubtedly involve the consequence that the earth is too sterile for the fecundity of man—for the possible increase of mankind; the earth can not forever yield food as fast as human beings can multiply; neither in this case nor in any other has provision been made for the unlimited gratification of any human propensity. Not even the most amiable instinct, not even the instinct of compassion, can be released from the control of prudence and conscience without entailing injury alike on the possessor and on society. Whether this be a ground for charging the Creator of the universe with a "miscalculation of means to ends" it is not for me to say; but the fact, I apprehend, is indisputable. If it be an "end" of creation that the human species should multiply unrestrained, the conditions under which man has been placed in the world do not, it must be confessed, seem well calculated for this purpose, and "the arrangements of the universe" do certainly, on *this* hypothesis, seem liable to the charge conveyed in the passage I have

---

[1] "'Wherever Providence brings mouths into the world, it will find wherewithal to feed them;' the profane form of the theory," says the Cambridge Don, "is that you ought to marry, because your relations can't let you starve."

quoted. For my part, I do not take this view of the "ends" for which "the arrangements of the universe" have been planned; but, as apparently Mr. Rickards does, I must leave him to reconcile it as he best can with those precepts of prudence directed against "over-population" which he has had the practical wisdom to inculcate.

LECTURE VIII.

OF THE THEORY OF RENT.

§ 1. OF those principles of Political Economy which have of late years been made the subject of controversy among economists, one of the most fundamental and important is the theory of rent, generally designated from the name of its ablest expounder, Mr. Ricardo. Mr. Rickards, of Oxford, some of whose objections to the doctrine of population, as taught by Malthus, I considered in my last lecture, is also an opponent of Ricardo's theory of rent. In the sixth lecture of his work on Population and Capital he remarks upon the close relation which exists between these two doctrines. "The arguments for both," he says, "rest on one and the same hypothesis." . . . "The same assumption—that of the diminishing productiveness of the land as compared with the undiminished power of human fecundity—forms the basis" of both theories.

Substantially I take this to be a correct statement of the case, and I am quite prepared to stake the truth of the doctrines in question upon the issue thus set forth. But, before adverting further to Mr. Rickards's objections, it will be desirable first to understand what the doctrine of rent is, as well as its proper limitations.

The object of a theory of rent is to explain the fact of rent, and the conditions which determine its rise and fall. In order, therefore, to judge of the theory, we must form a clear and definite idea of the fact of which it is designed to afford the explanation. The fact, then, which the theory of rent is adduced to explain is the existence in certain branches of industry of a permanent surplus value in the product, beyond what is sufficient to replace the capital employed in production, together with the usual profits which happen to prevail in the country. Thus a farmer, after replacing the circulating stock employed in cultivating his farm with the usual profits, and reserving, besides, interest on such capital as he may have sunk in outlay of a more permanent kind, finds that the proceeds of his industry still leave him an element of value. This element of value, if he be merely the occupier of his farm, goes to his landlord; or should he during the continuance of his lease be able to retain a portion of it, he will at all events on its termination be compelled by the competition of other farmers to hand it over to his landlord. On the other hand, if the farmer be himself the proprietor of the land which he tills, the sum in question will of course accrue to him along with his other earnings. In the same way the patentee of a successful invention, on selling the produce of his industry, finds himself also in possession of an element of value over and above what is sufficient to replace the cost of production, together with the ordinary profits. Now it is this surplus value, whether derived from agricultural or from manufacturing operations, whether retained by the producer or handed over to the owner of the productive instrument, which constitutes " rent " in the economic sense of that word, and the existence of which is the fact to be accounted for.

You will observe, I say "in the economic sense of the word," because this is one of those cases in which the necessity under which political economists are placed of using popular phraseology in scientific discussions has led to much confusion of ideas and perplexity of reasoning. The term "rent" is in popular language applied to the revenue which the proprietor of any article derives from its hire. Such a revenue, however, may owe its existence to different causes. The rent, *e. g.*, which a landlord receives from a farmer for the hire of his land, is derived from a surplus value in the proceeds of the farmer's industry beyond what will cover the expenses and profits of his farm. On the other hand, the building-rent of a house represents no surplus value of this kind. It is not any thing in addition to the ordinary profit, but is simply the ordinary profit or interest which the builder of the house receives on the capital which he has sunk.[1] There may, indeed, be fluctuations in the

---

[1] It will perhaps occur that the rent of land may equally be regarded as the interest of the landlord's capital sunk either in the purchase or improvement of his estate. So far as the rent paid by the tenant is the consequence of improvements made in the land, the case is no doubt analogous to that of building-rent, and the payment which the landlord receives in consideration of such improvements is properly regarded as the returns on the capital which he has sunk. But with regard to the remainder, the same explanation is not available. The payment of this by the tenant is not a consequence of the landlord's purchase of the land (in the same way as the increase in his rent, in consideration of improvements, is a consequence of these improvements): on the contrary, the money paid for the purchase of the land is a consequence of the rent. Farmers do not pay rent *because* landlords have invested money in the purchase of their estates; but landlords invest money in this way *because* farmers are willing to pay rent. If landlords had obtained their estates for nothing, as many have so obtained them, farmers would not the less pay rent; on the other hand, if, owing to any cause, corn fell permanently in value, rents would fall, whatever might have been the amount of the purchase money given for estates.

returns upon building speculations, as upon any other speculations—the speculators receiving sometimes more, sometimes less, than average profits; but there is in this case nothing like what occurs in the case of agricultural rent—a permanent surplus beyond what is sufficient to indemnify the capitalist. The existence of this surplus, then, is the problem which the theory of rent has to solve; and the question is, what are the causes to which it owes its existence, and what are the laws which regulate its amount?

Several theories have at different times been advanced in explanation of rent. That which was given by the French economists, and which, to a certain extent, was adopted by Adam Smith, traced the phenomenon to the superior productiveness of agricultural industry—to the positive fertility of the soil. Between agricultural industry and manufacturing, commercial, and other kinds, it was argued, there is this difference—that in the former alone is there a positive addition made to the commodity which forms the subject-matter of the industry. The manufacturer alters and adapts his material to some new use. The merchant transfers the article of his trade from the scene of its production to the place where it may be required. But the agriculturist alone employs the matter of his work in such a way as to lead to a positive increase in its quantity. Nature, it was said, co-operates here with human effort, and there consequently arises in agriculture a *produit net*, or " rent," which has no place in other fields of human effort. But, passing by other obvious objections to this theory, it suffices to consider that, whatever be the fertility of the soil and the abundance of the crop, the existence of a surplus value in the product depends not on these circumstances alone, but also upon the price paid for the commodity, in order to see that it fails to solve the problem of rent. It offers no explanation of the causes which regulate the price of agricultural produce. It gives no account of the fact that this price remains constantly high enough, not only to replace to the farmer the expenses of his outlay with the usual profits, but to yield a revenue besides to the owner of the soil.[1]

Adam Smith's contribution to the doctrine of rent as left by the Physiocrats consisted in the statement that the demand for human food was always, and the demand for other kinds of agricultural produce was generally, so great, that either could command in the market a price which was more than sufficient to indemnify the farmer, and that the surplus value naturally went to the landlord. This, however, still left the problem unsolved, and moreover implied an incorrect view of the laws of value; since, in the case of a commodity like corn, which may be produced in any quantity required, the price at which it sells does not, except during short intervals, depend on the extent of the demand for it, but on the cost of its production. An increase in the demand for a manufactured article, *e. g.*, generally leads, as soon as the

---

[1] M. Courcelle Seneuil claims that the true theory of rent was perceived by the Physiocrats, and quotes a passage from Turgot's work, "Observations sur le Mémoire de M. de St. Péravy," which shows that Turgot recognized the fact of the "diminishing productiveness of the soil;" but there is nothing in the passage to show in what way this fact connects itself with the phenomenon of rent. I can not hold, therefore, that the solution of the problem of rent is among the great services rendered by this distinguished philosopher to economic science.—See "Traité d'Économie Politique," par J. G. Courcelle Seneuil, tome i. pp. 179, 180.

supply has had time to adjust itself to the change, to a fall in the price, owing to the circumstance that manufactured articles are generally produced at less cost when produced on a large scale. The demand for cotton goods has probably been decupled in the course of the last half century, but this has simply resulted in a decupled supply produced at a cheaper cost and sold at a proportionately lower price. How does it happen, then, that the demand for human food does not operate in the same way? If, indeed, food were a strictly monopolized article, if only a limited quantity of it could be produced, we might understand how an increase of demand for it might permanently keep up its price above the cost of its production. But though land be a strictly monopolized article (at least in old countries), food is not so, since the quantity of food which may be raised from a limited area of land, though not infinite, is indefinite; and the maximum has never yet been reached, or nearly reached, in any country, and probably never will. The question, therefore, again recurs—how does it happen that the increased demand for food does not operate in the same way as the increased demand for clothes or shoes or hats, or other manufactured articles? How does it happen that the price permanently remains at such a point as to leave a permanent surplus value over and above what is requisite to pay cost of production with the usual profit? This is a question which Adam Smith failed to answer; and he consequently failed to solve the problem of rent.

The first writer who gave the true answer to this question was, I believe, Dr. Anderson, in a work published in 1777; but it remained for Ricardo fully to perceive the

I

importance of the principle involved, and to trace its influence in its various bearings on the laws of the production and distribution of wealth.

The answer to the question is as follows:

Agricultural produce is raised at different costs, owing to the different degrees of fertility of different soils; owing also to this, that, even of that corn which is raised on the same soil, the whole is not raised at the same cost. Now in order that that portion of the general crop of the country which is raised at greatest expense be raised —that is to say, in order to induce the cultivation of inferior lands, and the forcing of superior lands up to such a point as shall secure to the community the quantity of food required for its consumption—the price of agricultural produce must rise at least sufficiently high to indemnify with the usual profits the farmer for this— the least productive—portion of his outlay. If the price were not sufficient for this, the farmer would withdraw his capital from the production of that portion of his crop which is raised at greatest expense, and would invest it in some other business in which he had a fair prospect of average profits.[1] Now there are never two

---

[1] It will, perhaps, be said that the farmer would not withdraw his capital under the circumstances; that, being liable to his landlord for his rent, he will get the most he can out of his land, whatever be the price of agricultural produce. I hold, however, that a capitalist farmer (and it is only to such that the reasoning applies) would certainly do nothing of the kind. If he have made a bad bargain, and undertaken to pay rent for land of such indifferent quality that the produce at the current prices will not replace his capital with the ordinary profits, it will be much better for him to put up, once for all, with the first loss, to allow his land to lie waste, and to turn his capital into some employment in which it *will* yield him ordinary profits, than to continue throwing good money after bad by farming at a loss. And this is practically what every farmer does whose lease

prices for the same article in the same market. It is nothing to the consumer what may be the cost at which the article is raised; he simply looks to getting what he requires as cheaply as he can. If, therefore, the price of agricultural produce be such as to cover with ordinary profits the cost of that portion of the general crop which is raised at greatest expense — and I have shown that it must be this at least—it will be *more than sufficient* to cover with ordinary profits the cost of that portion which is raised at less expense. There will, therefore, be on all that portion a surplus value over and above what is sufficient to replace the capital of the farmer with the usual profit; and this surplus value is the precise phenomenon of rent which it is the purpose of the theory to account for.

§ 2. Such, briefly, is the theory of rent as taught by Ricardo. When you have thoroughly mastered this principle, you will find that you have the key to some of the most important problems of economic science. The doctrine, however, is one which is peculiarly liable to misconception; it has been and, I regret to say, is still the subject of much controversy. It may be well, therefore, to state in somewhat greater detail than I have yet done the grounds on which it rests, and to advert to some of the principal consequences which flow from it.

And, in the first place, what are the assumptions on

---

comprises lands too poor for profitable cultivation. He simply does not cultivate such land. Instead of employing his surplus capital in the unprofitable cultivation of such portions of his farm, he allows them to lie waste, and invests his spare cash in trade, in railway stock, or in some other enterprise which promises average profits.

which the theory of rent is founded? It assumes, first, that of the whole agricultural produce of the country, those portions which in the market are sold at the same price are not all raised at the same cost; and, secondly, that the price at which the whole crop sells is regulated by the cost of producing that portion of it which is produced at greatest expense. If these two points be granted, the existence of a surplus value, or, as we may call it, " economic rent," is a logical necessity which it is impossible to evade; and if we take further into account the motives which actuate farmers in hiring and landlords in letting their land, we shall see that it is equally a logical necessity that, under the action of competition, this " economic rent" should pass to the proprietor of the soil. The least consideration will make this evident. If corn be raised at different costs, and if the price be such as to cover with ordinary profits the cost of the most costly portion, it can not but be *more than sufficient* to cover with ordinary profits the cost of less costly portions. In the case, therefore, of all agricultural produce raised at *less* than the greatest cost, there must arise a " surplus value." And it is equally clear that this must be appropriated by the landlord. For, though farmers who had leases would be able during the currency of these leases to retain any new increments of " economic rent" that should arise, on their expiration they would stand on the same footing as the rest of their class. If, under these circumstances, they retained the " economic rent," the rate of profits in farming would be largely in excess of the rate in other occupations. Such an occurrence could not fail to attract increased capital to agriculture, and to lead to a competition for farms, which could only find its natural termination when agricultural and other profits were brought to a level—a point at which the whole "economic rent," or surplus value, would be transferred to the landlord.

I think, therefore, I am warranted in saying that, if the two assumptions which I have stated be granted, the theory of rent taught by Ricardo follows as a necessary consequence. We must, therefore, consider what are the proofs of these assumptions.

First, then, I say that, of the whole agricultural produce of the country, those portions which sell at the same price are not all raised at the same cost; that is to say, that a given barrel of wheat, barley, or potatoes of a certain quality is not raised at the same cost as every other barrel of wheat, barley, or potatoes of the same quality, and therefore commanding the same price. And this surely is a proposition that scarcely requires serious proof. To deny that some portions of the general crop of the country are raised at less cost than others is to deny that some soils are more fertile than others, is to deny that the county of Meath is more fertile than the county of Galway—the meaning of "more fertile" being that a given amount of labor and capital expended thereon produces a greater result. The fact, however, if seriously questioned, is, like all the axiomatic truths of Political Economy, susceptible of direct proof. The proper ultimate criterion in this case would be actual physical experiment on the soil. Farmers do, in fact, perform the experiment, and the result is sufficiently evidenced by the higher rent which they are content to pay for some lands than for others.[1] I think, therefore,

---

[1] Vide ante, p. 51, *note.*

we are warranted in assuming as an incontrovertible
fact that the whole agricultural produce of the country
is, taking the same kinds and qualities, not raised at the
same cost.[1]

But, secondly, the price at which the whole crop sells
is determined by the cost of producing that portion
which is produced at greatest cost.   It is not, of course,
meant by this that the market price of corn always accurately corresponds with the cost of this portion.   As
was explained on a former occasion,[2] when it is said that
cost regulates price, what is meant is that this is the point
which the price constantly tends to approach—the cen-
tre toward which it constantly gravitates.   This being
premised, it will not be difficult to prove that the price
of corn is determined by the cost of producing the most
costly portion of the general crop.   It is clear that the
price must at least be sufficient to cover this cost with
the ordinary profit.   If it were not, there would be no
inducement to farmers to continue the production of this
portion : a farmer will not continue permanently to produce corn at a loss.   Before he invests his capital in his

---

[1] One would suppose that this fact, so obvious when stated, could not
long have escaped the attention at least of "practical men."   Yet it was
a Committee of the House of Commons, who piqued themselves on their
practical knowledge, that reported that a price of 100s. to 105s. the quarter for wheat was necessary to enable farmers to continue the cultivation
of their land—less than this not being a "remunerative price;" as if the
necessary cost of raising corn were some fixed quantity, independent of
the character of the soil on which it is raised, or of the point to which cultivation may be forced upon it.   On the other hand, it was reserved for a
"theorist" (Ricardo, in his tract on "Protection to Agriculture") to discover that corn may be grown not only in the same country but on the
same soil at different costs, and that, therefore, the "remunerative price"
will vary with the state of agriculture.

[2] Vide ante, p. 106.

business, he will consider whether he has a fair prospect of receiving the ordinary returns on it; if he has not, he will not invest it. But if the price can not permanently be less than is sufficient to cover with ordinary profits the cost of this portion, it is equally certain it can not permanently be *more* than sufficient to do this.

This will appear when we consider the following facts: That between the worst and the best lands there are soils of every possible degree of fertility: some on which by dint of high culture corn might be raised, but at such a cost that it would not replace the capital expended in raising it; others in which, though the returns might replace the capital, they would not yield a profit; others, again, in which the returns would yield a profit, but less than an average profit; and others still in which the returns will just replace the capital expended with average profits, and no more; and when we consider, further, that no soil at present in cultivation yields as much corn as it might be made by higher cultivation to yield; that in forcing the soil there is a point at which the returns replace with ordinary profits the capital expended, and no more, and beyond which, if cultivation were pushed, though it would lead to an increase of produce, yet this increase would not be sufficient to replace the outlay with the ordinary profit: in a word, that there is a point up to which it is profitable to cultivate, and beyond which it is not profitable to cultivate —a fact from which it results that even on the most fertile soil the cost of production may attain any height, however great. Now if these several considerations be borne in mind, it will be seen that the price of corn will not, for any long time, remain at a higher rate than is sufficient to cover with ordinary profit the cost of that portion of the general crop which is raised at greatest expense ; for, were it more than this, the extraordinary profit would at once stimulate cultivation ; rich lands would be farmed more highly, and lands of a less fertile quality than before would be brought under tillage ; and the process would continue till either by an increased supply the price was brought down to the cost of production, or through the increasing expense of cultivation the cost of production rose up to the price.[1] It follows, therefore, that as the price of corn can not remain for any length of time at a *lower* point than is sufficient to cover the cost with ordinary profits of raising the most costly portion, so neither can it permanently remain at a *higher* point than is sufficient for this purpose. The extent to which cultivation shall be carried in bringing poor soils under the plow, and in forcing the better qualities—what Dr. Chalmers calls "the extreme margin of cultivation"—must be determined by the wants of society; but, wherever that margin may be, whatever in the actual state of agriculture may be the cost of raising the most costly portion of the general crop, this will be the regulator of price—the point which it will constantly tend to approach.

I trust I have now established to your satisfaction the two assumptions on which rest Ricardo's theory of rent. Let me once more repeat them : Of the total quantity of agricultural produce raised in a country, different portions, quality for quality, are raised at different costs of production ; and, secondly, the price at which agricult-

---

[1] Vide ante, p. 106, *note.*

ural produce sells is determined by the cost of producing that portion of the general crop which is raised at
greatest expense. From these two assumptions, or, as I
may now call them, facts, it results, as I have already
shown, that in the cultivation of agriculture in a country
like England a "surplus value" arises; while, from the
principles of human nature brought into play in the
traffic for farms, it follows that this "surplus value" must
go in the form of rent to the proprietor of the soil.

§ 3. The theory of rent just set forth explains the phenomenon of rent in the case of all lands on which agricultural produce is raised at less than the greatest cost
at which it can be profitably produced; and this description applies to the great mass of agricultural land
in a country like England; but it explains it in this case
only. It has accordingly been objected to the theory,
first, that it fails when applied to new colonies in which
none but the best lands, in point of fertility and situation,
are under cultivation; where, therefore, since all the
corn is raised at one and the same cost, there could, according to Ricardo's theory, be no surplus value; and,
secondly, that it fails to account for the payment of rent
in the case of the worst lands under cultivation in every
country, on which the whole produce is raised at the
maximum of cost, as well as in the case of those lands
which are too poor for cultivation, but which nevertheless pay rent.

It can not be denied that the facts are as the objection
states them to be; but, if you have fully seized what I
said on a former occasion as to the kind of proof by
which economic laws are established or refuted, you will

understand that this by no means amounts to an invalidation of the theory.   That theory, as I have shown you, rests on facts quite as certain as those which are urged against it, and of far wider reach and more important bearing.   What the objection proves is, not that the theory is unfounded, but that, over and above the phenomena which it accounts for, there are others, not perhaps properly described as "economic rent," but of a nature closely allied thereto, for which it does not account. It is a case, in short, and at the utmost, of what in physical science is called "a residual phenomenon," and is to be treated in the same way—namely, by looking out for some new cause or principle adequate to explain the residual fact.[1]

---

[1] On the recurrence of a "residual phenomenon" in physical investigations it always becomes a question whether the theory, which leaves the fact unexplained, is to be retained, accompanied with the hypothesis of some concurrent cause undetected to which the residual phenomenon may be ascribed, or whether the theory should be wholly rejected.   But in economic reasoning no such questions can arise.   The grounds of the distinction have been pointed out in the third lecture ; they are to be found in the different character of the proof by which ultimate principles in physical and economic science are established.   The proof of a physical theory always, in the last resort, comes to this, that, assuming it to be true, it accounts for the phenomena ; whence it follows that the occurrence of a "residual phenomenon" in physical researches necessarily weakens the proof of the laws which fail to explain it, and, if such exceptions become numerous and important, may lead to the entire rejection of the theory. On the other hand, it is always regarded as the strongest confirmation of the truth of a physical doctrine, when it is found to explain facts which start up unexpectedly in the course of inquiry.   (Vide Appendix C.)   But the ultimate principles of Political Economy, not being established by evidence of this circumstantial kind, but by direct appeals to our consciousness or to our senses, can not be affected by any phenomena which may present themselves in the course of our subsequent inquiries (the proof of the existence of such phenomena consisting also in appeals to our consciousness or to our senses, and therefore being neither more nor less cogent than that of those ultimate principles) ; nor, assuming the reasoning

Let us take, *e. g.*, the case of a new colony for every acre of land in which government exacts a rent before it permits occupation. Here we will suppose that none but the best lands are cultivated, and that all the corn produced in the colony is raised at the same cost. Under these circumstances it is undeniable that rent, or what has been called such, has been frequently, and still is in many cases, paid. It is certain, however, that farmers, whether in a new colony or elsewhere, will not engage in the production of corn as a commercial speculation if they have not a reasonable prospect of obtaining such a rate of return on their investment as prevails in the place where they reside. If an emigrant capitalist can make thirty per cent. by employing men at gold digging, he will not be content with twenty per cent. on growing maize. Consequently, before a farmer will consent to pay the rent demanded by government for colonial land the price of corn must be such as to indemnify him for this imposition. Here, then, it is evident that the excess of price beyond what cost of production requires —which excess of price goes to the government in the form of rent—is a result of the monopoly of the land enjoyed by the state.

Again, take the other case to which I have referred—

---

process to be correct, can the theory which may be founded on them. We have here no alternative but to assume the existence of a disturbing cause. In the case before us, *e. g.*, under whatever circumstances rent may be found to exist, this can never shake our faith in the facts that the soil of the country is not all equally fertile, and that the productive capacity of the best soil is limited; nor weaken our confidence in the conclusions drawn from these facts that agricultural produce is raised at different costs, and that in the play of human interests this will lead to the payment of rent to the proprietor of the superior natural agent.

the case of rent paid for the worst lands under cultivation; or, a more extreme case still, the case of rent paid for the worst lands in the country, too poor for cultivation of any kind. With respect to the former, it may perhaps be said that the payment of rent is more apparent than real. It rarely happens that the lands comprised in one farm under one holding do not contain several varieties of soil. An average rent is struck over the whole, and the bad land appears to pay as much as the good. In point of fact, however, it is the extra profit derived from the better qualities of land that makes it worth while paying rent at all. The payment of rent on the inferior sorts is nominal merely; so that we are justified in saying that virtually no rent is paid for such lands.

It will be said, however, that rent of some kind is paid for every acre of land in Great Britain, however barren and worthless. This is true; but where this is so, land is not taken as a commercial speculation. The rent which may be obtained for land too poor for cultivation is a consequence of the fact that land, even when not available as an instrument for the production of wealth, is still an object of desire as a means of enjoyment, and, being also limited in supply, becomes an article of wealth. Mountains in Wicklow and in the Highlands of Scotland, on which a barrel of oats could with difficulty be raised, will nevertheless let at a good round rent as game-preserves; and even where there is not vegetation enough to shelter a hare or a grouse, such lands are yet not to be had for nothing, since, at the least, they minister to the pride of proprietorship. In this case, as in that of the unoccupied lands of a colony, the rent which the owner is enabled to exact is simply a consequence of the monopoly which he enjoys.

I have mentioned two cases of rent in which the phenomenon is not explicable on the theory of Ricardo. I shall now mention another—the case of the rent paid to the patentee of an invention for the use of his patented process, where this process has superseded all others. Here the article produced is all produced at the same cost ; nevertheless the patentee is enabled to exact a rent for the hire of his invention. It is evident that the so-called rent, or value in excess of cost and profit, is due in this case to the same cause as in that just considered —namely, monopoly. There is indeed this limitation on the monopoly of a patentee, that the article to which his patent applies may still be produced in the ordinary way ; but, subject to this limitation, he has a strict monopoly of the production of the article. He will consequently refuse to sell it except at such a price as shall leave him, not only ordinary profit, but a surplus value besides ; or, if he should not choose to engage in the production himself, he will not permit the patented process to be used except on condition that the person using it shall pay him some valuable consideration for its use, leaving it to the producer to indemnify himself in the price of the article.

It thus appears that, besides the causes of rent embraced in the theory of Ricardo, there is another—namely, monopoly—from which also the phenomenon may take its rise. When any of the agents or instruments indispensable to the production of an article is monopolized, the person in possession of the monopoly may refuse to allow the article to be produced, except on his own terms ;

consequently, under such circumstances the article, whatever it may be, will not be produced unless the price of it be sufficient to enable the producer to comply with these terms, besides getting the ordinary remuneration for himself.

§ 4. Perhaps it will here occur to some of my readers that the introduction of two distinct principles into the theory of rent involves an unnecessary complication; and that—land being a monopolized article—the simple condition of monopoly in connection with the play of supply and demand would suffice to account for the phenomenon in all cases whatever. A little reflection, however, will show that such a generalization is not admissible. Agricultural rent, as it actually exists, is not a consequence of the monopoly of the soil, but of its diminishing productiveness. If it were not for this latter condition, though rent might exist, it would, both as regards its amount and the laws of its rise and fall, be governed by principles wholly different from those which determine the actual phenomenon in its more familiar form. Further, it is a mistake to suppose that, in order to the existence of " economic rent," land should belong to one class of persons, and be cultivated by another, or even that it should be a marketable commodity. So long as land is not uniform in quality, and so long as its productiveness diminishes when its capacity of yielding produce has been forced beyond a certain point, so long agricultural products will be raised at different costs, and so long there will arise that surplus value in such products, over and above the average returns obtainable in other branches of industry, which, as I have shown, is the essence of " economic rent." For the existence of rent, therefore, monopoly and the play of supply and demand are not necessary; nor do they suffice to account for the phenomenon in the form in which we most commonly find it.

As the causes determining rent in the ordinary case of agricultural rent are different from those which determine it in the special cases to which I have called attention, so also are the consequences in the distribution of wealth different in the two cases. In the ordinary case of agricultural rent, the relation of rent to price is not that of cause to effect, but of effect to cause; rent, that is to say, is the consequence, not the cause of the high price of agricultural products. If, *e. g.*, the property of landlords were confiscated, the price of corn would not be affected, since the price must still be sufficient to cover the expense of producing the portion of the general crop which is raised at greatest cost, and, as I have already shown, it is not more than sufficient to do this at present. The effect of such a measure would not be to abolish " economic rent," but simply to transfer this element of value from the owners to the cultivators of land.

On the other hand, in the special cases of rent referred to—in the case, *e. g.*, of the unoccupied lands of a colony, rent is not the effect, but the cause of price. In Great Britain the price of corn rises *because the government demands a rent.* In the ordinary case, the landlord demands a rent *because the price of corn is high*. If in the former case the government were to abandon its exactions, the price of corn would fall proportionally; in the latter, the high price, not being due to the exactions of the landlord, would not be affected by their abandonment.

The same is true of all cases of rent, where rent is the consequence of monopoly, *e. g.*, in the case of a patentee. The value of an article produced by a patented process is sufficient to afford a rent to the patentee after covering the expenses and profits of the producer. But abolish the monopoly of the patentee, and the competition of producers would at once bring down the price by the amount of the rent; in other words, the surplus value would disappear; and this is, in fact, what always happens on the expiration of the term of a patent.

But again, rent, according as it results from the principles noticed by Ricardo, or from monopoly, is governed by different laws. With regard to the former phenomenon—what I may describe as "Ricardian" or "economic rent"—we can now have no difficulty in stating the conditions which determine its amount. As we have seen, it consists in the surplus value appertaining to agricultural produce over and above what suffices to indemnify the farmer for his outlay on the terms of remuneration current in the country. This surplus value manifestly depends on two conditions: on the one hand on the price of agricultural produce, on the other on the quantity of such produce obtainable from a given area of land. We may, therefore, formulate the law of agricultural rent as follows: The price of agricultural produce being given, agricultural rent—that is to say, the "economic rent" accruing from agricultural land—will vary directly with the productiveness of agricultural industry—this productiveness being the function of two variables, viz., the natural fertility of the soil and the skill with which labor is applied to it; or, the productiveness of agricultural industry being given, rent will vary directly with the price of produce.

On the other hand, rent, where it is a consequence of monopoly, depends simply on the demand for and supply of the article. The amount of rent which the English government may exact for unoccupied lands in Australia is controlled by nothing but its own will on the one hand, and on the other the strength of the desire and the ability to purchase on the part of the colonists. In Great Britain consumers would be able and willing to pay ten times or twenty times the present price for bread rather than do without it; and landlords, we may venture to assume, would have little scruple about exacting higher rents, had they the power to do so; but just as the competition of farmers operates to enable landlords to appropriate that portion of the returns of land which is in excess of ordinary profit, so, on the other hand, the competition of landlords among themselves renders the exaction of more than this impracticable. That landlords should be able to keep up the price of corn by holding out for higher rents would require a combination of the whole body, which, without a law to enforce it, it would be impossible to carry into effect. But what landlords, from their number and rivalry, are unable to do, government, wielding the concentrated power of the community, has no difficulty in doing. If, *e. g.*, government chose to exclude foreign corn from a new colony, it might, by demanding a higher rent, force up the price of corn to any point short of the extreme limit which consumers were able and willing to pay. Rent, therefore, is in such case governed not by the necessary cost or costs of producing corn, but simply by the need and ability to purchase of the consumer on the one hand, and by the disposition of the owner of the natural agent on the other—or, according to the usual phraseology, by demand and supply.

We have arrived, therefore, at the following conclusions : Agricultural rent, to which alone the theory propounded by Ricardo is applicable, differs from the other cases to which I have adverted—first, with reference to its cause: the cause of agricultural rent being the different costs at which agricultural produce is raised, while the other cases of rent are due to the principle of monopoly ; secondly, it differs in the consequences to which it leads : agricultural rent having no effect upon price, while the rent that results from monopoly leads to a rise of price in proportion to the rent; and, thirdly, it differs in the laws by which it is governed: the rent which results from monopoly being governed, like other cases of monopoly, solely by the principles of demand and supply, while the rise and fall of agricultural rent depend on the relation between the productiveness of agricultural industry and the price of agricultural produce.

It is most important to observe the distinction between these two phenomena of rent, to the confusion between which the objections which have been advanced by various writers against the theory of Ricardo owe whatever plausibility they possess. So important indeed is the distinction that, were we framing a new nomenclature of Political Economy, I should prefer confining the term rent to the case of agricultural rent, as contemplated by Ricardo, considering those other cases of rent which are the consequences of monopoly as coming under the head of taxes on commodities, to which they are strictly analogous. In a certain sense, the sovereign authority of the state may be said to have a monopoly of every article of production, inasmuch as it may refuse to permit its production except upon such conditions as in its sovereign pleasure it chooses to enact. The British government, *e. g.*, imposes a tax upon malt, and refuses to allow malt to be made except on condition that for every bushel of barley malted a certain sum be paid into the exchequer. The consequence is that the price of malt rises to such a point as is sufficient not only to cover the expenses and profits of production, but to leave over and above a surplus value which goes to the government as the malt-tax. If government were to raise the tax higher, the price would rise higher; if it were to abolish the tax, the price would fall proportionally. It is evident this is in all respects analogous to the case of a rent on the unoccupied lands of Australia, and is attended with consequences of precisely the same kind. The revenue derived from this source, therefore, would be more properly considered as a tax on raw produce than as rent. In the same way, the rent derived from a patented process has all the attributes of a tax. It springs from the monopoly of the patentee; it is regulated by his discretion; and it constitutes an addition to the natural price of the article. The word "tax," however, is generally confined to the exactions of the state; and the laxity with which the term "rent" is applied to every form of revenue derived from articles let to hire is probably too inveterate to be corrected. It is all the more important, therefore, that the distinction in facts should be carefully noted.

§ 5. In the opening of the present observations I called attention to the ground of objection taken by Mr.
Rickards to the doctrines which I have been examining
in this and the last lecture, viz., that they "both rest
upon the same assumption—that of diminishing productiveness of the land as compared with the undiminished
power of human fecundity." My object in recurring
to this question now is not to offer any further arguments
in support of a position which I conceive has been already sufficiently established, but to avail myself of the
reasoning of Mr. Rickards in illustration of what it has
been the object of these lectures to prove—viz., the influence which mistaken views of the character and method
of economic science have exercised in producing those
discrepancies of opinion in relation to fundamental doctrines to which I adverted in the outset.

Mr. Rickards denies that "the diminishing productiveness of agricultural industry" is a fundamental economic law; and having quoted Mr. Mill's statement of the
law, with his explanation that it is constantly neutralized
in a greater or less degree by "an antagonizing principle" designated by Mr. Mill "the progress of civilization," proceeds to remark :[1]

"With regard to the alleged *law* of production, herald-
ed forth by this author as 'the most important proposition
in Political Economy,' I confess myself unable to understand on what foundation it is supposed to rest. A *law*
of the social system, if I rightly understand the expression,
can only be deduced from ascertained facts; it is a rule
founded on a plurality of instances to the same effect.
We are entitled, therefore, to ask, When and where has

---

[1] "Population and Capital," pp. 135, 136, 137.

such a law been found in operation? What period or what country can be referred to in which the rule has been or is now in force? Certainly it does not hold good in England—a country where, undoubtedly, though there is still great room for improvement, 'men have applied themselves to cultivation with some energy, and have brought to it some tolerable tools;' a country, too, in which the peculiar density of its population operates constantly to bring fresh soils into cultivation. But in England it seems to be admitted, or, at all events, it can be abundantly proved, that if we take any two periods sufficiently distant to afford a fair test, whether 50 or 100 or 500 years, the productiveness of the land relatively to the labor employed upon it has progressively become greater and greater. . . . But the manner in which Mr. Mill accounts for the admitted aberrations from his supposed law of production presents to my mind still greater difficulties. The law, according to him, is counteracted or suspended by an agency which is 'in habitual antagonism' to it; and this agency is, in brief phrase, 'the progress of civilization.' Are, then, the only exemplifications of this 'law' to be found in countries in which civilization is not advancing? Is the law one which never co-exists with a state of social progress? But, surely, it is such a state as this that all our reasonings, as political economists, presuppose; this is 'the natural course of things,' as Mr. Senior justly says, 'for it is the course for which nature has fitted us.' Suppose civilization not advancing, and all those phenomena of the social system which economists have studied and described become reversed—population falls off, combination of labor gives place to isolation, machinery to manual toil, communications are cut off, exchange is impeded, and labor of every kind, not only agricultural but manufacturing also, becomes less and less productive. This is, no doubt, true; but this can hardly be what Mr. Mill means by 'the most important proposition in Political Economy,' for it is one which operates only in an abnormal state of human affairs, and gives place to a converse rule whenever the manifest design of Providence and destiny of our species are fulfilled—that is, by the progress of civilization. It is that progress which, by its manifold effects and influences, direct and indirect, as set forth by Mr. Mill himself, tends to confer, as wealth and numbers multiply, an increasing productiveness both on the soil and on every other field of human industry. This is, indeed, a 'law' which, so far as experience hitherto informs us, has never failed to operate, and of which we may, therefore, reasonably infer that its beneficient operation is still likely to continue."

Mr. Rickards's conception of "an economic law" is, as appears from this passage, something essentially different from that of Mr. Mill, and, as might be expected, the views of these economists as to the kind of evidence applicable to the proof of such a law are equally at variance.

An "economic law," according to Mr. Mill's view, represents the influence which a particular cause (in the present instance, the physical character of the soil) exerts on some of the phenomena of wealth; and, agreeably with this view, his method of establishing the law consists in a reference to facts which prove the physical character in question, and then in reasoning on the premises thus obtained. According to Mr. Rickards, on the other hand, an "economic law" is not an assertion respecting the influence of any one cause, or even the combined influence of any number of known and definite causes, but a statement of the order in which events have actually taken place — these events being the result of a vast variety of causes, more or less or not at all known; and this being his conception of an economic law, he naturally has recourse to history or statistical tables in order to establish it. The one is a statement respecting a tendency now existing, the ultimate proof of which is to be sought in the character of man or in physical nature : the other is a statement respecting an historical fact, and, as such, must of course ultimately rest upon documentary evidence. In whatever sense, therefore, each may be determined, it is plain that neither can be taken in refutation of the other, since it merely amounts to the assertion of a wholly different proposition. In deciding, therefore, between Mr. Rickards and Mr. Mill, we have to consider, not which proposition is true, for there is nothing incompatible in the two doctrines, but which, regard being had to the ends of Political Economy — the explanation of the phenomena of wealth—is to the purpose.

Now touching that " law," " which, so far as experience hitherto informs us, has never failed to operate " (so says Mr. Rickards)—" the progress of civilization " —it is obvious that, as I observed when replying to the same argument on a former occasion,[1] such a statement affords no explanation of any phenomenon connected with the production and distribution of wealth, but is itself the expression of a complex and difficult phenomenon which it is the business of the political economist to explain. To bring forward this as a final result in economic speculation—to deprecate all analysis of the causes on which the so-called " law " depends (and this is what Mr. Rickards's argument would require)—is simply to abandon all pretensions to solving

[1] See ante, p. 180.

the problems of wealth — is to give up at once the cause of Political Economy as a branch of scientific research.

On the other hand, the influence of the physical qualities of the soil, as expressed by the law of its diminishing productiveness in Mr. Mill's sense, is a principle most important with reference to the objects of Political Economy, and quite essential in enabling us to understand the actual phenomena presented by agricultural industry—a principle which, taken in conjunction with the various agencies included under the expression " progress of civilization," explains, among other things, that general tendency to a fall of profits and rise of rent, which, though frequently and sometimes for long periods interrupted, is nevertheless one of the most striking circumstances connected with the material interests of advancing communities. It is to be observed that there is nothing in what I have quoted from Mr. Rickards, nor, I may add, in any part of his work, which can properly be said to impugn the correctness of this explanation. In terms, indeed, he denies some of the propositions on which it is founded, but in terms only ; when we come to examine his meaning, we find that it has reference to a wholly distinct question. His remarks, so far as they are pertinent, consist in an attempt to ridicule the idea of any explanation.

" Mr. Mill's law," he says, " has not yet come into operation." [1]   And why ?   Because, forsooth, it has been counteracted by a law of an opposite tendency.

---

[1] Page 141.

"It has been postponed (to say the least) by the habitual antagonism of various causes." I am most anxious not to misrepresent Mr. Rickards, but it appears to me that the only possible inference to be drawn from this language is that he refuses to admit the existence of a law or tendency unless the operation of this law be perfectly free from all obstructing or counteracting influences; in short, that he regards the mutual counteraction of opposing forces as an amusing but unsubstantial fiction of philosophers.

It is scarcely necessary to say that such views go directly to impugn the whole received system of inductive philosophy. If, for example, such objections are to be listened to, how is the first law of motion to be established? The objector might say, "When and where has such a law been found in operation? certainly it does not hold good in England." So far from its being true that a projectile once set in motion will proceed forever in the same direction with unimpaired velocity, we know that the best minié rifle will not send a ball more than a couple of miles, and that it is almost immediately bent out of its direct course into one nearly resembling a parabola. "Does the law of motion only operate in an abnormal state of human affairs?" If the physical philosopher were to explain that the natural tendency of the law was "habitually counteracted" by the antagonizing force of gravity, he would be met by the retort that this mode of accounting for "the admitted aberrations from the supposed law presented to the mind still greater difficulties." The law of motion, according to the physical philosopher, "is counteracted or suspended by an agency

K

which is in habitual antagonism, and this agency is, in brief phrase," the law of gravitation. "Are then the only exemplifications of this law to be found in countries in which" the law of gravitation does not exist?

It is, I say, scarcely necessary to insist that such a line of reasoning is wholly inconsistent with the received logic of the inductive sciences; and, if admitted, the structure must fall. The diagonal of a parallelogram must no longer stand for the resultant of the forces represented by the sides. The facts of the ascent of a balloon through the air, of the rise of the mercury in the Torricellian tube, must be considered as a "refutation" of the law of gravity; the gyrations of a boomerang as a disproof of the first law of motion. The neutral salt, just because it is neutral, no longer contains the acid. Friction has no existence and no effect, because it does not bring the vehicle to a stop. The advance of a ship against wind and tide is a proof that there is no wind or tide. The progress of the world in civilization is a proof that there are no passions in human nature, and no laws in the physical world which tend to impede it. In short, the notion of "habitual antagonisms" is to be at once exploded. The attempt to resolve complex uniformities into simple principles — in Baconian language, "the interpretation of nature"—is to be abandoned, and we are henceforward to content ourselves with the rough statistical results.

According to the views here indicated of the character and method of the science, Political Economy is plainly identical with the statistics of wealth and population, and this is a view of Political Economy which is probably widely entertained, and, for aught I know, may include some Professors among its supporters. If this view, however, is to be accepted, the pretensions of the study, as a means of analyzing and explaining the causes and laws of which the facts presented by statistical records are but the result, must be given up. We may indeed give to the empirical generalizations which are to be found at the bottom of our statistical tables, and which are " founded on a plurality of instances to the same effect," the sounding title of "laws of our social system ;" but if such empirical generalizations are to be regarded as ultimate facts, if every attempt at further analysis is to be met by ridicule of the idea of causes being in " habitual antagonism," and by simple re-assertion of the complex phenomenon to be explained, then, however we may persist in retaining the forms and phrases of science, the scientific character of the study is gone ; and Political Economy has no longer any claim to be admitted among those departments of knowledge of which the business is not only to observe, but to interpret nature.

It appears to me, however, that there is nothing in the phenomena of wealth which takes them out of the category of facts in explanation of which the method of analysis and deductive reasoning may be applied. I have endeavored to show that while on the one hand we labor under much disadvantage, as compared with those who investigate physical phenomena, in being precluded from experiment, and in having to deal with facts of an extremely complex and fluctuating character ; on the other hand we possess peculiar advantages in deriving our premises either directly from our consciousness, or from physical facts easily ascertainable, instead of being obliged to elicit them by long and intricate courses of inductive reasoning. It has been by following the method indicated in this view of the problems of wealth that such truths as Political Economy has yet brought to light have been established; and by steadily prosecuting our inquiries in the same direction by the same road, I, for one, feel confident that most of the difficulties which now beset economic questions may be overcome, and that still more important truths may be discovered.[1]

---

[1] I may, perhaps, be permitted to refer to my Essay, "Political Economy and Land"—in the volume "Essays in Political Economy, Theoretical and Applied"—for a discussion of some aspects of the problem of rent not treated in the foregoing lecture, and in particular for an examination of the effects of different social conditions in causing a divergence of the actual rent paid by cultivators from the "economic rent" as defined by the theory of Ricardo.

APPENDICES.

APPENDICES.

APPENDIX A.

IF, not confining myself to economists of established position and reputation, I were to include every writer on economic questions, there is not a single doctrine within the range of the science that could be said to be undisputed. A late writer (1857), *e. g.*, Mr. Macleod, in a work entitled "The Theory and Practice of Banking," proposes to make a complete *tabula rasa* of Political Economy (which he considers as "almost a branch of mechanics;"—"all sciences," he tells us, being "questions of force and motion"), and to reconstruct it, taking as its basis certain notions of credit and capital, which he claims to be the first to have evolved, and his title to the discovery of which will probably pass unchallenged. This writer thus delivers himself: "We do not hesitate to say that there is not a single writer on Political Economy who has given a correct account of them [the laws of wealth]; and more especially what has been written lately is the result of the most extraordinary misconception of the nature of the thing, the most profound ignorance of the details of business clothed in language so palpably self-contradictory and inaccurate as to excite nothing but surprise" (vol. ii., Introduction, p. lviii.). . . . " THE TIME HAS COME WHEN ALL POLITICAL ECONOMY MUST BE RE-WRITTEN. Every error in thought and language, which confused and retarded all the other inductive sciences, now deforms and obscures monetary science. There is hardly an expression in common use among writers on the subject which is not totally erroneous" (p. lxxx.).

The weapons by which Mr. Macleod proposes to demolish the present edifice of the science would seem to be vituperative epithets. Here are a few examples of his method. Ricardo's theory

of rent he brands as a " prodigious delusion." Mr. Mill's nomenclature implies " the most ludicrous misconception," etc. Of the
doctrine that cost of production regulates value, he says that " no
more stupendous philosophical blunder ever infected the principles of any science." In the next sentence it is called a " tremen-
dous fallacy," and further on a " pestilent heresy." Mr. Tooke's
distinction between currency and capital exhibits " a profound
misconception of the whole nature of monetary science—" . . .
" one of the most profound delusions that ever existed." A passage quoted from Colonel Torrens is " nothing but a series of blun-
ders and absurdities;" his statements are " simply ridiculous;"
while in another place he confounds together in one sweeping
category " Mr. Ricardo, Mr. McCulloch, Mr. John S. Mill, Mr. Sam-
uel Jones Loyd, Colonel Torrens, Mr. Norman, Sir Robert Peel, and
Sir Archibald Alison," as the propounders of every species of logical fallacy.

The cause of the failure of Political Economy hitherto, Mr. Macleod tells us, is " that no writer who has yet handled it possessed
the indispensable qualifications for success." These qualifications
the writer then not obscurely hints have been incarnated for the
first time in the person of the author of " The Theory and Practice
of Banking." Among the requisites for success, one would imagine a competency to write the English language, and a capacity
to understand the views of previous writers before denouncing
them, would be included. How far these are included among
Mr. Macleod's qualifications the reader may judge from the following examples.

First, to take a specimen of this author's defining power. " Capital," he tells us, " is the circulating power of commodities " (vol.
ii., Introduction, p. xlvii.). When Mr. Macleod tells us elsewhere
that " the object and function of capital is to circulate commodities," he uses language which, however objectionable and repug-
nant alike to scientific requirement and to popular usage, has at
least the merit of being intelligible. Again, when he says that
" capital and credit constitute the circulating medium," though
the expression implies a fundamental misconception of the nature
of the agencies in question, we may yet guess at what he means.
But when he says that " capital is the circulating power of com-

modities," if he does not mean to attribute to commodities a faculty of locomotion, he uses language which is capable of conveying no idea whatever; yet this, he tells us, is "the original primary and genuine sense of capital" as distinguished from "the secondary or metaphorical sense." Let us suppose that Mr. Macleod meant by the expression, "circulating power of commodities," what assuredly the language does not convey, viz., the power which circulates commodities, even this will not help him. From his remarks elsewhere it is plain that he meant to designate money and credit. Now money and credit are not the *power* which circulates commodities, any more than air is the power which transmits sounds, or language the power which communicates ideas. The *power* which performs all these things is the human will; money and credit in the one case, air and language in the other, being the media or instruments by which the several ends are accomplished. But, without entering into the metaphysical question, let us ask what would be thought of a writer who should describe air as "the transmitting power of sounds," or language as "the communicating power of ideas?"

Take another example of Mr. Macleod's scientific precision. He thus lays down the criterion of a true principle, "*Every true formula, or general rule, must bear on the face of it all the elements which influence its action*" (p. lxv.), *i. e.*, which influence the action of the formula! One may guess at the idea which Mr. Macleod intends to express; but the words as they stand are destitute of meaning. Take another case. In p. lxi., etc., Mr. Macleod objects to the law of "cost of production regulating value," because it is inapplicable to "all cases where the same cost of production produces articles of different qualities." Will Mr. Macleod inform us how "cost of production" can "produce articles?" In another passage he writes thus, "Alone of all the political sciences, its phenomena [*i. e.*, the phenomena of monetary science] may be expressed with the unerring certainty of the *other* laws of nature" (p. xxxv.). If I may venture to conjecture the meaning of this remarkable passage (which has a curiously Hibernian ring about it), possibly what Mr. Macleod *meant* to say was that the phenomena of monetary science may be expressed with the same unerring certainty as the phenomena of the other inductive sciences—a

K 2

thought, one would imagine, which might be conveyed without severely taxing the resources of the English tongue.

These are a few specimens, and by no means unfavorable ones, of Mr. Macleod's ordinary scientific style;[1] they are taken, it will be observed, from that portion of his work in which accuracy of expression would be found, if it were to be found at all—namely, from his definitions and statements of general principles.

I have called attention to them, not only because of the importance of accuracy of thought and language in economic discussion, but because this writer, not content with pronouncing a general and sweeping condemnation on all preceding writers on Political Economy, has singled out for special denunciation their defects in regard to precision of language, a quality on which it is evident he peculiarly values himself. Thus his anger passes all bounds against Mr. Mill, because that author states at the opening of his treatise that it is no part of his design " to aim at metaphysical nicety of definition, when the ideas suggested by a

---

[1] As a specimen of his style when he is less restrained by scientific considerations, take the following : " Some Political Economists pretend that the rules of the science are not applicable to extreme cases. An extremely convenient cover for ignorance, truly ! Such arguments only prove the incapacity of those who use them. If an architect had miscalculated the strength of the materials of his columns, and his building came tumbling down, and he were to run about, crying out, ' It is an extreme case ; the laws of mechanics do not apply to it !' the world would set him down as a fool. If an engineer, whose boiler was to burst from bad workmanship, were to say that it was an extreme case, and that the laws of heat did not apply to it, he would be set down as a fool. In both these cases people would say that the architect and the engineer did not pay sufficient attention to the laws of nature. They would not say that the laws of nature paled before the incompetence of man. Those Political Economists who say that the laws of their science are not applicable to extreme cases are just like such an architect or such an engineer. Such a doctrine is the mere cloak of their own incompetence and ignorance. A false theory may account well enough for a particular case, like an engine may be at rest whose piston is crooked, whose wheels and cranks are all out of order. But the test of a well-finished engine is to work smoothly ; it must be set in motion to test it properly. Just so with a theory ; it must be worked—it must be set in motion. If it be true, like a well-fitting engine, it will work smoothly, it will explain all phenomena in the science ; if it be not true, like a badly fitting engine it will crack, split, break in all directions.

" Mr. Macaulay has used a similar line of argument with great skill and effect," etc.

term are already as determinate as practical purposes require."
For this Mr. Mill is charged with deliberately adopting "all the
loose phraseology of the public"—with seeking to "found a system on the loose babble of common talk." After the few samples
given above, probably most readers will prefer the laxity of Mr.
Mill to the rigid accuracy of Mr. Macleod. *Mallem, mehercule, er-
rare cum Platone.*

But a word with regard to Mr. Macleod's capacity of understanding the authors whose writings he treats so contemptuously.
A large portion of the introduction to his second volume is devoted to an attempt to controvert the received doctrine, which attributes to "cost of production" a governing influence on the value of certain classes of commodities. "Political Economy," he
says, "can never advance a step until this arch-heresy be utterly
rooted out." Well, what is his contradiction of the "arch-heresy ?" Here it is, given in capitals: "VALUE DOES NOT SPRING FROM
THE LABOR OF THE PRODUCER, BUT FROM THE DESIRE OF THE CON-
SUMER. To allege that value springs from the labor of the producer is exactly an analogous error in Political Economy to the
doctrine of the fixity of the earth in Astronomy" (p. lxiv.).

Granting that the analogy is perfect (though, for one, I am unable to perceive it), will Mr. Macleod inform us who has said that
"value springs from the labor of the producer?" His so-called
"refutation" was more particularly addressed to the views of Mr.
Ricardo and Mr. Mill. In the second paragraph of Mr. Ricardo's
great work, he writes as follows: "Utility, then, is not the measure
of exchangeable value, *although it is essential to it.* If a commodity were in no way useful—in other words, if it could in no way
contribute to our gratification—it would be destitute of exchangeable value, however scarce it might be, or *whatever quantity of labor might be necessary to procure it.*" The first sentence in Mr. Mill's
chapter "On Demand and Supply in their Relation to Value" is as
follows: "That a thing may have any value in exchange, two conditions are necessary. *It must be of some use*—that is, it must conduce to some purpose, *satisfy some desire.* But, secondly, the thing
must not only have some utility, there must also be some difficulty
in its attainment."

Mr. Macleod's refutation of the doctrine that "cost of production regulates value" is, therefore, simply a refutation of his own extravagant misconception of it. If any further evidence be necessary to show this, take the following passage, in which an objection is taken to the ordinary limitation which is given to this doctrine—"because for it to indicate price correctly, even in that one instance, it requires this essential qualification, that the supply should be unlimited" (p. lxi.). Now if the supply were "unlimited," the article could have no exchange value whatever. What the authors who have maintained this doctrine have stated, and what possibly Mr. Macleod intended to say, was that the articles, of which the value is regulated by cost of production, are only those which may be freely produced in any quantity required; but Mr. Macleod can see no distinction between this and an "unlimited supply."

When a writer thus shows an entire inability to comprehend the meaning of authors of such remarkable perspicuity and power of expression as Mr. Ricardo and Mr. Mill (for I will not suppose that he intentionally misrepresents them), his competency for the task he has undertaken of reconstructing the science of Political Economy, may be imagined. It is, of course, unnecessary to notice his "arguments" in refutation of the doctrine in question. It will be time enough to do so when he shows that he understands the principle he assails.

APPENDIX B.

THE limits of economic investigation contended for in the text, though, as has been seen, not in keeping with the theories of some distinguished economists, have, in the actual development of the science, been all but universally observed. As a rule, every economist, so soon as an economic fact has been traced to a mental principle, considers the question solved, so far as the science of wealth is concerned; just as he considers it equally solved when he has traced such a fact to a physical principle. Though Adam Smith has not formally discussed the question, his view may be inferred from the following passage : " The division of labor from which so many advantages are derived is not originally the effect of any human wisdom which foresees and intends that general opulence to which it gives occasion. It is the necessary though very slow and gradual consequence of a certain propensity in human nature which has in view no such extensive utility—the propensity to truck, barter, and exchange one thing for another. Whether this propensity be one of those original principles in human nature, of which no further account can be given, or whether, as seems more probable, it be the necessary consequence of the faculties of reason and speech, *it belongs not to the present subject to inquire*" ("Wealth of Nations," book i. chap. ii.). In other words, he distinctly declines to "explain the laws of mind" under which division of labor takes place; regarding them as facts not to be explained, but to be taken notice of and reasoned upon, in precisely the same way as in a subsequent chapter he notices the physical qualities of the precious metals—their portability, durability, divisibility, etc.—as physical facts to be taken account of, in order to understand the general adoption of them for the purposes of money. He no more attempts to explain the mental principles which lead to division of labor than he attempts to explain the physical principles which render the precious metals suitable as a medium of exchange. In both cases, in the language of Mr. Senior, "he is satisfied with stating their existence."

The only writer, so far as I know, who has, *in practice*, transcended the limits indicated and observed by Adam Smith, is Mr. Jennings in his "Natural Elements of Political Economy." Not content with assuming mental principles as premises to be reasoned upon, in the same way as physical principles are assumed and reasoned upon, Mr. Jennings regards the explanation of the laws of mind as coming properly within the province of the political economist; and, agreeably with this view, his book is devoted to an analysis of the principles of human nature, psychological and physiological, which are brought into action in the pursuit of wealth. Thus, having resolved the operations of industry into certain movements of muscles and nerve-fibre, he proceeds "to inquire what is the *modus operandi* of the mental influence which actuates these organic instruments;" and this *modus operandi* having been analyzed, and the mental elements of the process ascertained, he makes these the basis of the division of industrial actions. These he divides as follows, viz.: firstly, those which are "marked simply by the law of former co-existence"—of which he gives the examples of "digging, threshing, rowing, sawing," etc.; secondly, those which are "marked by the application of judgment to the merely memorial trains of thought," *e. g.*, those of "superintendents, inspectors," etc.; thirdly, those which are "marked by the application of the law of resemblance to those processes of thought," *e. g.*, those of "painters and sculptors;" and, fourthly, those which are "marked by the further application of judgment to resemblance," *e. g.*, those of "judges, legislators," etc. (pp. 115 to 117).

Hitherto the nomenclature of Political Economy has been framed with reference to the phenomena of wealth, or the mode of its production and distribution. Mr. Jennings, taking a different view of the nature of economic science, defines and classifies on wholly different principles. Thus, "consumption" he defines as "that class of human actions in which the instrumentality of the afferent trunks of nerve-fibre is predominant." The sensations which attend upon consumption, again, he divides "into two classes, according as they are conveyed by the nerves of common sensation, or by the nerves of special sensation." In the former class are comprised "sensations of resistance," of "temperature," . . . "sensations consequent on the gratification of appetite," etc. In the latter, viz., those conveyed by nerves of special sensation, are included the charms of "color, of "form," and of "sound;" . . . "the luscious taste which the palate derives from elaborate substances, in which sapid properties are joined with congenial odors, and diffused through substances agreeable to the touch."

If Political Economy is to be treated in this way, it is evident it will soon become a wholly different study from that which the world has hitherto known it. It is undoubtedly true, as Mr. Jennings remarks in his preface, that the subject-matter of Political Economy represents the complex result of mechanical, chemical, physiological, and biological laws, together with the laws of mental and political philosophy; but I can not think that it follows from this that "each of the more complex of these subjects, being governed by all the laws which govern every subject of inferior complexity, in addition to its own peculiar laws, ought not to be examined until the difficulties which surround each of these less complex subjects have been surmounted progressively and seriatim." Were this rule rigorously enforced, and were no one to be allowed to matriculate as a political economist till he had mastered all the less complex sciences, including mechanics, astronomy, chemistry, magnetism, electricity, general physics, physiology, biology, together with mental and political philosophy, the practice would certainly be attended with the advantage of effecting a very extensive reduction in the economic ranks; if, indeed, with the exception of Mr. Jennings himself, any should be found capable of passing the terrible ordeal. But I confess that I am quite unable to see the necessity of making such impossible demands upon the human intellect. Surely, to recur to the example taken from Adam Smith, it is possible to perceive that division of labor and exchange facilitate the production of wealth, without deciding whether the disposition which leads to this course of conduct be an original or derived faculty; or to

understand the advantages which the precious metals offer as a
measure of value and medium of exchange, though we may be
wholly ignorant whether they are simple or complex substances,
or appear at the positive or negative pole of the battery. Or, to
take an example from Mr. Jennings's book, I confess I am quite
unable to see what new light is thrown upon the causes which
determine the laborer's condition, by his telling us that during
" production the instrumentality of the efferent trunks of nerve-
fibre is predominant," while during " consumption " it is " the
afferent trunks of nerve-fibre which prevail." So long as the result is the same, so long as human beings possess the same ener-
gies, require the same subsistence, and are influenced by the same
motives, the economic laws of wages will be the same, though
they had neither " afferent " nor " efferent " trunks of nerve-fibre
in their bodies. Even were the encyclopædic knowledge demanded by Mr. Jennings easily attainable, it appears to me that
nothing but confusion and error could arise from extending economic inquiry beyond the limits which have hitherto been observed. Take, *e. g.*, the division of industrial operations which I
have quoted above from Mr. Jennings, founded upon his analysis
of the mental principles engaged—what is the *economic* value of
this classification ? What light does it throw on the phenomena
and laws of wealth ? Mr. Jennings places in the same class of
" industrial operators " judges and legislators, because the actions
in which they engage are " marked by the application of judgment and resemblance to the merely memorial trains of thought ;"
but, economically considered, if it be desirable to class them at
all, judges are far more widely separated from legislators than
from " superintendents," or from " diggers, threshers, rowers, or
sawyers," who are placed in distinct classes ; judges being highly
paid officers, while legislators (at least in Great Britain), instead
of being paid, are obliged to pay handsomely to be allowed to
exercise their functions. If a judge be paid more highly than a
digger, it is not because the exercise of the functions of the latter
involve only " memorial trains of thought," while the exercise of
those of the former involve besides the faculties of judgment and
of perceiving analogies—this, economically considered, being an
accident ; but because the persons who are qualified to perform

the functions of a judge are much fewer than those who are qualified to dig ; and the reason the former are more scarce is partly because the requisite natural faculties are more rare, and partly because the expense necessary to their due cultivation is considerable.

Classification will, I presume, be more or less perfect in proportion as it is founded upon those qualities in the objects of it which, with reference to the ends of the science, are essential ; but a classification based upon an analysis of the psychological or physiological operations which take place in the production or distribution of wealth will not divide producers or distributors according to their economic importance, but according to circumstances which, economically considered, are purely accidental.

APPENDIX C.

THE following passage from Dr. Whewell's "History of the Inductive Sciences" contains so elegant an example of the logical process by which the great generalizations in physical science are established, that, with a view to illustrate some occasional references to the line of reasoning pursued in physical investigations which occur in the text, I am induced to extract it:

"When we look at the history of the emission-theory of light, we see exactly what we may consider as the natural course of things in the career of a false theory. Such a theory may, to a certain extent, explain the phenomena which it was at first contrived to meet; but every new class of facts requires a new supposition—an addition to the machinery; and as observation goes on, these incoherent appendages accumulate, till they overwhelm and upset the original frame-work. Such was the history of the hypothesis of solid epicycles; such has been the history of the hypothesis of the material emission of light. In its simple form, it explained reflection and refraction; but the colors of thin plates added to it the hypothesis of fits of easy transmission and reflection; the phenomena of diffraction further invested the particles with complex hypothetical laws of attraction and repulsion; polarization gave them sides; double refraction subjected them to peculiar forces emanating from the axes of crystals; finally dipolarization loaded them with the complex and unconnected contrivance of movable polarization; and even when all this had been assumed, additional mechanism was wanting. There is here no unexpected success, no happy coincidence, no convergence of principles from remote quarters: the philosopher builds the machine, but its parts do not fit; they hold together only while he presses them: this is not the character of truth.

"In the undulatory theory, on the other hand, all tends to unity and simplicity. We explain reflection and refraction by undulations; when we come to thin plates, the requisite 'fits' are already involved in our fundamental hypothesis, for they are the length of an undulation: the phenomena of diffraction also require such intervals; and the intervals thus required agree exactly with the others in magnitude, so that no new property is needed. Polarization for a moment checks us; but not long; for the direction of our vibrations is hitherto arbitrary—we allow polarization to decide it. Having done this for the sake of polarization, we find that it also answers an entirely different purpose— that of giving the law of double refraction. Truth may give rise to such a coincidence; falsehood can not. But the phenomena became more numerous, more various, more strange; no matter: the theory is equal to them all. It makes not a single new physical hypothesis; but out of its original stock of principles it educes the counterpart of all that observation shows. It accounts for, explains, simplifies the most entangled cases; corrects known laws and facts; predicts and discloses unknown ones; becomes the guide of its former teacher, observation; and, enlightened by mechanical conceptions, acquires an insight which pierces through shape and color to force and cause " (vol. ii. pp. 464–6).

Such has been the process by which the great inductions in physical investigation have been established. In economic inquiry (as I have shown in my third lecture) this circuitous method is unnecessary, the ultimate facts and assumptions being susceptible of direct proof.

THE END.